Anabolic Steroid Abuse in Public Safety Personnel

Anabolic Steroid Abuse in Public Safety Personnel

A Forensic Manual

Brent E. Turvey

Stan Crowder

AMSTERDAM • BOSTON • HEIDELBERG • LONDON
NEW YORK • OXFORD • PARIS • SAN DIEGO
SAN FRANCISCO • SINGAPORE • SYDNEY • TOKYO
Academic Press is an imprint of Elsevier

Academic Press is an imprint of Elsevier
32 Jamestown Road, London NW1 7BY, UK
525 B Street, Suite 1800, San Diego, CA 92101-4495, USA
225 Wyman Street, Waltham, MA 02451, USA
The Boulevard, Langford Lane, Kidlington, Oxford OX5 1GB, UK

Notices
Knowledge and best practice in this field are constantly changing. As new research and experience broaden our understanding, changes in research methods, professional practices, or medical treatment may become necessary.

Practitioners and researchers must always rely on their own experience and knowledge in evaluating and using any information, methods, compounds, or experiments described herein. In using such information or methods they should be mindful of their own safety and the safety of others, including parties for whom they have a professional responsibility.

To the fullest extent of the law, neither the Publisher nor the authors, contributors, or editors, assume any liability for any injury and/or damage to persons or property as a matter of products liability, negligence or otherwise, or from any use or operation of any methods, products, instructions, or ideas contained in the material herein.

ISBN: 978-0-12-802825-4

British Library Cataloguing-in-Publication Data
A catalogue record for this book is available from the British Library.

Library of Congress Cataloging-in-Publication Data
A catalog record for this book is available from the Library of Congress.

For Information on all Academic Press publications
visit our website at http://store.elsevier.com/

This book has been manufactured using Print On Demand technology. Each copy is produced to order and is limited to black ink. The online version of this book will show color figures where appropriate.

DEDICATION

The mission of law enforcement, "to protect and serve," must not be comprised by the illicit use of drugs by those individuals sworn to uphold the law. Law enforcement officers are guardians of a sacred trust, and as such, must be beyond reproach.

Daley and Ellis (1994; p. 3)

CONTENTS

FOREWORD

I spent several years, in the early part of my career, working in an undercover capacity infiltrating organized drug trafficking organizations. Anabolic steroids were the most difficult cases to uncover and the penalties were not severe enough to act as a deterrent to the enormous profits available. I observed clandestine labs for their production, as well as prescription steroids being abused by criminals and law enforcement alike. The use, abuse, and trafficking of illegal anabolic steroids was not taken seriously by law enforcement agencies, public safety leadership, prosecutors, and judges. Additionally, most law enforcement leaders or administrators either did not know about the signs and dangers of steroid use or they did not care. This was and is an unacceptable response due to ignorance of the product and its proliferation into our law enforcement, win-at-all-costs, culture.

The "must-win" culture that has been promulgated within law enforcement and public safety has placed inordinate pressures, including peer pressure, on those who enter these professions. Though prevalent in all areas of public safety, the use and abuse of illegal anabolic steroids has appeared to rear its ugly head most often within the ranks of first-line officers, deputies, troopers, fire, rescue, corrections officers, and first responders from other emergency services. These folks are the ones who are placed in harm's way on a daily basis. The respect garnered from, and confidence conveyed by peers is paramount within these ranks; bigger is better. Conversely, someone who has excelled in the academic and operational acumen required to perform at an acceptable level, but performs marginally in the physical aspects, may draw consternation and suffer a lack of acceptance by others in their respective endeavor.

There has been a blind eye turned to this self-destructive and criminal behavior by public safety leadership for years. As with other abuses, such as alcohol or prescription medications, this too is another crutch that some public safety employees may turn to, without knowing the dangers, the potential for compromise and the inherent, yet hidden devastation it can cause in the lives of the abusers and their families. Self-medication has always been difficult to identify, unless or until one is made aware of the signs and dangers *prior* to falling into the depths of the issue. The abuser may feel that the potential for some ambiguous side effects, years down the road isn't enough to make him avoid the use of these products. The use and abuse of illegal anabolic steroids is still a form of self-medication in trying to become the biggest, the strongest or the fastest person on the squad. The abuse of anabolic steroids is just another form of this same old problem.

Without the benefit of "being armed" by the information and insight available in this publication, first responders would be more likely to be swayed by peers and uninformed "do-gooders" who would point the youngster in a direction that ultimately would cause the demise of their career ... if not their life. There is a powerful penchant in the first responder corps which pushes them to be the very best and perform at the highest levels in every aspect. With each new generation of folks entering these careers, the caliber of applicant and the competition for each vacancy becomes more pronounced. To some degree, this abhorrent behavior is a by-product of our own making by leadership being uninformed, misinformed, or not caring to be informed. It does not, however, excuse or forgive the action. Like all of the advances that have been made in public safety over the years, this too is a new opportunity to face and overcome an old problem that has manifested into a near epidemic.

To prosecuting attorneys and judges illegal anabolic steroids have been viewed as a low-priority crime that really doesn't have the "sex appeal" as a heroine trafficker or a cartel-related case. In reality, the proliferation of illegal anabolic steroid cases has quietly infiltrated all socioeconomic groups, including those that one might not expect ... public safety professionals. The information contained in this manual will educate and assist prosecutors and judges by bringing home the importance of seeking remedies, not just mediocre prosecutions of law enforcement and public safety professionals that would have little or no deterrent effect.

The content of this text has a multifaceted view of the problem, the detection, and the policy direction for public safety. I envision the text being most advantageous to investigators, supervisors, first responders, and public safety leaders and administrators. The usefulness for attorneys and judges educates those who can curb the scourge of illegal anabolic steroids beyond the potential for not only the malfeasance of abusers but also the prescription for corruption that can creep into an organization. I recommended this manual for reading for new recruits in the academy as a component of the health and wellbeing segments taught to new employees. I highly recommend this text and subject to the curriculum of *all* first responder organizations and their academies.

Captain Jeff Pearce, Spotsvania County (Virginia) Sheriff's Office

Bureau of Alcohol, Tobacco, Firearms, and Explosives, Retired

CHAPTER *1*

Introduction

In accordance with the *Crime Control Act of 1990* and the *Anabolic Steroid Control Act of 2004* (Federal Register, 2005), anabolic steroids are Schedule III Controlled Substances. In other words, it is a crime to possess, sell, use, or distribute these kinds of drugs outside of their narrowly prescribed medical purposes.[1] Despite this criminal prohibition, public safety personnel are commonly found within the community of anabolic steroid abusers.[2] Public safety personnel include those serving in police departments, fire departments, and emergency medical services. Abuse by law enforcement in particular is widespread, and often occurs in plain sight without significant consequence (Sweitzer, 2004).

This observation is not a revelation, least of all within the law enforcement community. There have been multiple warnings about the problem and the need for a genuine response over the course of the past three decades. Specific to anabolic steroid abuse, the literature has been blunt, and has documented the general failure of police agencies to take preventative or punitive action. This is when they acknowledge the problem at all.

The situation is that there are officers who want to bulk up and flex—commonly under the guise of gaining a physical "edge" or advantage over the criminals that they anticipate (DEA, 2004; James, 2007).

---

[1]Possession of anabolic steroids is generally a misdemeanor unless the intent to sell can be established. Then it becomes a felony. As we will discuss, the dealer—user model is common with these drugs, to finance what can be an expensive addiction.

[2]Other groups commonly associated with anabolic steroid abuse include professional and recreational athletes; military personnel; and celebrities/performers.

The solution for some is the illegal use of anabolic steroids because it is an easy way to get big fast. Add to this the reality that too many in public safety are (i) ignorant about the adverse side effects related to anabolic steroid abuse; (ii) encouraging themselves internally to maintain fitness and even use performance enhancers in order to achieve and maintain a physical edge; and (iii) generally unwilling to inform on, or arrest, fellow officers for the felony activity that necessarily accompanies anabolic steroid abuse when they benefit (in a variety of ways) from the image that it reinforces.[3] That is the place we find ourselves, and it is difficult for the ethical criminal justice professional to navigate. Hence the need for this manual.

1.1 THE LITERATURE

Almost 25 years ago, the illegal use and abuse of anabolic steroids by law enforcement personnel was described as a "serious problem" in the *FBI Law Enforcement Bulletin* (Swanson et al., 1991, p. 19). This was a groundbreaking effort which acknowledged, in its opening sentence, that "substance abuse among police officers is not new."[4] It was a call to action, aimed at raising officer awareness about the dangerous side effects and criminal consequences of anabolic steroid abuse. It also sought to highlight potential departmental liability in order to help administrators avoid it. It was full of helpful wisdom and important admonitions.

---

[3]Multiple active duty law enforcement officers from different parts of the United States reviewed this manuscript prepublication. They unanimously expressed that those in law enforcement understand the adverse side effects of anabolic steroid abuse very well. However, they felt that users chose to lie to themselves and others about it in order to rationalize their addictions.

[4]In particular, it mentioned the problem of alcoholism, which remains an area of study that has received little attention despite persisting as a corrosive but silent epidemic within the ranks of law enforcement.

Abuse of Anabolic Steroids

By
CHARLES SWANSON, Ph.D.,
LARRY GAINES, Ph.D.,
and
BARBARA GORE, M.S.

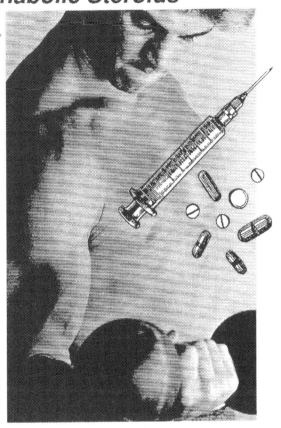

S ubstance abuse among police officers is not new. Alcohol abuse has long been recognized as a problem in police work. In fact, a study conducted in 1984 by the National Institute of Occupational Safety and Health revealed that 23 percent of officer respondents had serious drinking problems.[1]

Intensifying this problem is the increased use of illegal drugs by police officers. In recent years, drug abuse in law enforcement has garnered a great deal of attention.[2] Numerous individual cases of police officers using or dealing drugs have received nationwide publicity, and police officers in various ranks and assignments have been involved. However, one area of substance abuse that has been ignored, for the most part, is police officer use of steroids.

Anabolic steroid abuse by police officers is a serious problem that merits greater awareness by departments across the country. The adverse health conditions, both physical and psychological, that such abuse carries need to be dealt with in an informed manner. Because steroid use was originally tied to athletics and fitness conditioning, the abuse of these drugs can be overlooked by the law enforcement profession,

A few years later, two researchers from North Carolina (Daley and Ellis, 1994) got together and reviewed regional departmental drug testing policies. One was an academic and the other was an experienced law enforcement professional. They found that most police agencies at the time didn't require urinalysis for applicants, and most did not require random drug testing for active personnel. In other words, most had no mechanism for preventing, identifying, or managing drug-addicted police employees. They also concluded: "it is unlikely that individual police departments would find either the support or courage for recommending stronger [drug testing] policies" (p. 16). This despite the utter necessity for policy reform.

More recently, a 2004 report by the Drug Enforcement Administration served to remind that "Anabolic steroid abuse... has entered into the law enforcement community" (DEA, 2004, p. 1). This was a more mature and up-to-date effort meant to build on the FBI Law Enforcement Bulletin's admonitions back in 1991. Its mission was to educate law enforcement personnel, with the clear implication that the public safety community remained in the dark regarding the health problems and criminality associated with anabolic steroid abuse.

Subsequently, and in a response to the overall lack of action taken by law enforcement leadership, the International Association for Chiefs of Police (IACP) warned (Humphrey et al., 2008): "Rather than look back on what could be an embarrassing 'steroid era' of law enforcement—one in which the profession might be riddled with lawsuits, corruption, and claims of heavy-handedness—it is critical to address the current and future impact of this issue head-on." This was an excellent article that echoed many of the concerns raised in the three prior research efforts. Unfortunately, it falls flat with the conclusion that a reasonable remedy includes drafting legislation "disallowing the use of AASs by police officers unless a medical exception is granted."

The authors would agree with the IACP that, even now, something needs to be done. However, the action described above seems to miss the point that criminal prohibitions already exist; using anabolic steroids without a valid prescription is already a crime with harsh penalties, as will be discussed. Criminalizing it further won't change things if the police community is ignoring laws that are already on the books. And the fact that state and federal agencies have to step in and write articles explaining this a couple of times every decade is strong evidence that the problem will continue to be ignored by local law enforcement. At the very least it demonstrates that local agencies are not dissuading new hires from using what they ignorantly regard as beneficial performance- and image-enhancing drugs (a.k.a. PIEDs; discussed at length in Sweitzer, 2004).

1.2 RATIONALE

The authors have observed, through active casework and ongoing research, that anabolic steroid abuse by law enforcement and other public safety personnel is nationwide. In fact, the nature and frequency of steroid abuse scandals uncovered in association with US law enforcement agencies since 2004 suggests that the problem is getting worse (Perez, 2010).[5] Additionally, these scandals tend to demonstrate that local law enforcement agencies are routinely incapable of recognizing and resolving illegal steroid abuse by their own; they often handle things both incompetently and unlawfully. The authors have also observed that illegal anabolic steroid abusers in public safety are encouraged by the ignorance and inaction of supervisors, administrators, and the judiciary.

---

[5]One researcher referred to law enforcement use of anabolic steroids as "commonplace", while a DEA spokesperson referred to it as a "big problem" that cannot be ignored (Perez, 2010).

In light of this history, and the overwhelming evidence of steroid abuse as a feature of law enforcement subculture, the purpose of this work is to both educate and assist. It will help educate those in the criminal justice system as to the nature and illegalities of anabolic steroid abuse, with a focus on public safety personnel. It will also raise awareness regarding the pervasiveness of the problem, as it is both a systemic and nationwide phenomenon—not the result of individual or isolated "bad apples." Finally, it will address the consequences of anabolic steroid abuse to individual health, agency liability, and public safety. Particular attention will be paid to forensic issues (e.g., investigative, evidentiary, and legal concerns), in order to facilitate just and lawful outcomes when these crimes are suspected or exposed.

We have designed this work to serve as an investigative and forensic desk reference manual. It can be used by supervisors, chiefs, administrators, and policy makers when they are inevitably confronted with steroid abuse by law enforcement and other public safety personnel within their command or realm of influence. It can help to craft policy and direct related internal investigations. It can also help those investigating cases in relation to potential criminal and civil litigation—to include internal affairs investigators, criminal investigators, prosecutors, and civil attorneys. Currently, there is no other single comprehensive manual available on the subject to give these professionals informed direction.

1.3 CONCLUSION

Anabolic steroid abuse is a criminal act—a felony in many cases. The illegal use of anabolic steroids by public safety personnel is widespread, and the criminal justice community seems divided between not understanding the problem and denying that it is one. Whichever is true, there are those in the criminal justice system that are willing to break the law, ignore it, and even help suppress evidence of criminal wrongdoing when it comes to "juicing" by public safety personnel.

The seriousness of the problem cannot be understated. When public safety personnel engage in illegal anabolic steroid abuse, the following tends to be true:

1. They are violating the very laws that many of them are sworn to uphold and protect.

2. They are lying about it to others on job applications,[6] during official inquiries, and while under oath, violating any related oaths of truthfulness and integrity.[7]
3. They suffer harmful physical and mental side effects that jeopardize their fitness for duty.
4. They put the public that they are sworn to protect and serve in danger.
5. They lose the public trust, something that is vital for the effective functioning of any public safety agency.

In essence, those involved in related activity, or concealing it, become a party to fraud and public corruption. These themes will be explored and built upon throughout this work.

Case Example
Jefferson County Sheriff's Office, Colorado

In September 2013, a steroid and drug scandal that had been brewing inside the Jefferson County Sheriff's Office was finally made public. It involved at least five sheriff's deputies, but only one resignation and arrest. As reported in Maass (2013), the arrest and related details had originally been sealed by the court—meaning it was intentionally hidden from the general public:

Ryan Jordan, formerly a Deputy with the Jefferson County Sheriff's Department in Colorado, takes a "selfie" during one of his workout sessions. This picture was then posted to Facebook. In 2014, Jordan pled guilty to possession of a controlled substance after he was found to be in illegal possession of Oxycodone and Decabol (an anabolic steroid, a.k.a. Nandrolone Decanoate) to avoid a trial.

---

[6]Providing false statements and testimony in these contexts, including on government job applications, is typically a criminal offense. The specific applicable statutes are often spelled out on any official government documents to be signed, as a matter of course.

[7]Truthfulness and integrity are essential core traits of any public safety employee, especially for those who routinely write official reports and give sworn statements or testimony as part of their duties (California Crime Laboratory Review Task Force, 2009; Kleinig, 1996; Leonard, 1969; Marche, 2009; Stephens, 2006).

A veteran Jefferson County sheriff's deputy is due in court later this week following his arrest earlier this year for possession of anabolic steroids and oxycodone...

The previously unreported arrest of the deputy led to Jordan being allowed to resign from the Jefferson County Sheriff's Department where he had served for 20 years, most recently as a night shift deputy in the Jefferson County Jail.

According to court documents and law enforcement sources, the West Metro Drug Task Force raided Jordan's Arvada home on Jan. 8. There, investigators say they found Decabol, an anabolic steroid that is a synthetic derivative of testosterone, along with Oxycodone, a prescription pain reliever. Decabol is widely used by bodybuilders to increase muscle mass.

The search warrant in the case has been sealed since January. Jordan was charged with one felony count and one misdemeanor count...

Jefferson County Sheriffs Department officials say subsequent to the Jordan arrest four other deputies who worked in the jail alongside Jordan were called in and questioned about possible involvement in the use of steroids. But Sheriff Ted Mink says none of those deputies were suspended or disciplined. "We did look into that matter and there was nothing to substantiate their involvement with the procurement of steroids," Mink said.

Jordan, 47, worked for the sheriff's department since 1993, but was allowed to resign in April in the face of termination. Jordan, a military veteran, is listed as 6-foot-2 and weighs 225 pounds.

Mink called the steroid bust "disheartening" since he said Jordan was a good employee and had an impressive military career. He said there had been no previous indications of steroid use or "roid rage" from Jordan. "There were no complaints of excessive force or behavior that would indicate that. There was nothing in his file that would indicate that."

Mink said the county has a drug testing policy that would allow the sheriff's office to test a deputy for steroids if evidence suggested that was an issue.

In April 2014, former Deputy Jordan made a plea deal with local prosecutors. This happened just 1 week before his criminal trial was set to begin. The felony charge was dismissed, and "Jordan entered a guilty plea... to possession of a controlled substance, a misdemeanor"; he received 15 months probation (Maass, 2014).

Note that Jordan's former boss, Sheriff Mink, explained how the internal investigation into the other officers named found no evidence of "involvement with the procurement of steroids."[8] However, there was no mention as to whether these same officers were searched for possession of anabolic steroids, and/or whether they were required to submit to a urinalysis. These would have been obvious investigative steps. Moreover, had the overall results of this investigation been clean across the board, then this would have been made crystal clear in the Sheriff's statements to the press.

Until the full results of the internal investigation in this case are made public, it is unclear whether a complete investigation was conducted, and whether these other officers were given a pass to avoid further embarrassment to the department.

This case is fairly representative of a typical law enforcement response to the identification of an illegal anabolic steroid ring found operating within its own ranks: don't investigate what you don't have to; concede what you must while the media is reporting; report publicly that you are running an internal investigation that is ongoing to protect agency image (but avoid any steps that might lead to other abusers or the sources of their illegal drugs); and hope that the FBI and DEA don't take an active interest while the public forgets.

Case Example
Christy Mack and "War Machine"

It is no secret that many of those in public safety enjoy sports, some to the point of emulating their favorite sports figures. It is also no secret that many professional athletes have been found abusing anabolic steroids, often in association with arrests for domestic violence. This includes those participating in the Mixed Martial Arts (MMA), who generally cannot achieve their level of bulk and fitness without the illegal use of anabolic steroids.

In accordance with its rise in popularity, many law enforcement agencies and police unions have encouraged their officers to "train, train, train" in MMA. This in order to more effectively respond to, and

---

[8]It is common for law enforcement agencies to end their investigation into officers abusing anabolic steroids without publicly identifying how those officers obtained their illegal drugs. In any other kind of investigation into illegal drugs, this would be the next step and perhaps even the sole reason for making the arrest—to identify and arrest the dealers.

incapacitate, those in the general public with MMA training (Phillips, 2008). The dangers of this emulation, and training response, should be evident—it lays the groundwork for illegal anabolic steroid abuse by setting a standard that is almost impossible to meet without it.

With this in mind, consider the case of War Machine. On August 8, 2014, Jonathan Koppenhaver, a mixed martial arts fighter (e.g., MMA, UFC, XFC) also known by his stage name "War Machine," is alleged to have unlawfully entered the home of his estranged girlfriend, Christy Mack (a.k.a. Christine Mackinday). At the time, Ms. Mack (a popular adult film star) was at home in bed with another boyfriend, Corey Thomas.

War Machine claims that he was there to propose marriage (to be clear, Koppenhaver has legally changed his name to War Machine). Ms. Mack and Mr. Thomas told a very different story to the police, as did their respective injuries. According to the police report in this case, both were attacked by War Machine while in Mack's home, in her bed, at 0130 hrs. Both were physically assaulted and threatened with death. In addition, Mack was sexually assaulted in a violent manner that was intended to be degrading. The full police report is provided here for reference.

Adult film star Christy Mack and her boyfriend, Jonathan "War Machine" Koppenhaver, during happier times. His t-shirt reads "I DO ALPHA MALE SHIT."

LAS VEGAS METROPOLITAN POLICE DEPARTMENT
DECLARATION OF WARRANT/SUMMONS
(N.R.S. 171.106)
(N.R.S. 53 amended 07/13/93)

EVENT: 140808-0491

STATE OF NEVADA)   JOHNATHAN KOPPENHAVER
                      ss: ID# 2519422
COUNTY OF CLARK)   DOB 11-30-81

Detective D. TOMAINO P#8278, being first duly sworn, deposes and says:

That he is a police officer with the Las Vegas Metropolitan Police Department, being so employed for a period of 10 years, assigned to investigate the crime(s) of (1 COUNT) BATTERY W/ SUBSTANTIAL BODILY HARM, (1 COUNT) STRANGULATION, (2 COUNTS) BATTERY W/ SUBSTANTIAL BODILY HARM DV-RELATED, (1 COUNT) KIDNAPPING DV-RELATED, 1 COUNT) OPEN AND GROSS LEWDNESS DV-RELATED, AND (1 COUNT) ATTEMPTED MURDER DV-RELATED committed on or about AUGUST 8TH, 2014, which investigation has developed JOHNATHAN KOPPENHAVER as the perpetrator thereof.

THAT DECLARANT DEVELOPED THE FOLLOWING FACTS IN THE COURSE OF THE INVESTIGATION OF SAID CRIME TO WIT:

1. On 8-8-14, Christine Mackinday became the victim of (1 Count) Attempt Murder DV-Related, (1 Count) Battery W/ Substantial Bodily Harm DV-Related, (1 Count) Kidnapping DV-Related, and (1 Count) Open and Gross Lewdness DV-Related. On 8-8-14, Corey Thomas became a victim of Battery with Substantial Bodily Harm. Both were victimized at 3496 Pueblo Way, Las Vegas, Nevada 89121. The incident was investigated by LVMPD Patrol Officers S. Schumaker P# 8743, and M. Truax P# 13752 and was documented under event numbers 140808-0491 and 140808-0494.

2. The incident occurred in the City of Las Vegas, County of Clark, State of Nevada.

3. Christine Mackinday and Johnathan Koppenhaver have been dating for 15 months. Corey Thomas states he is also in a dating relationship with Christine Mackinday for 2 to 3 months.

4. LVMPD Event 140808-0491. On Friday August 8th 2014 at 0450 hours I officer S. Schumaker P#8743 and Officer M. Truax P#13752   responded to Sunrise Hospital in reference a domestic disturbance that occurred at 3496 Pueblo Way Las Vegas, NV 89121.

Upon arrival contact was made with victim Christine Mackinday DOB 05/09/1991. Both of Mackinday's eyes were swollen shut. Mackinday had bruising around her eyes and dry blood around her nose and mouth. Mackinday also had swollen lips and was missing two of her teeth. Mackinday was asked what happened and she stated her boyfriend Jonathan Koppenhaver whom she has been dating for 15 months came over to her residence at approximately 0130 hours while she was in her bedroom in bed with her friend Corey Thomas. Koppenhaver slapped Mackinday and then began beating up her friend Thomas.

Thomas left the residence and Koppenhaver began accusing Mackinday of cheating on him. Koppenhaver began going through Mackinday's text messages and then began punching her in the face with his fist causing her to fall to the ground. C Mackinday stated once she was on the ground Koppenhaver started to kick her causing bruising to her right rib and left thigh.

Mackinday stated Koppenhaver threatened to kill her and took her cell phone so she was unable to call police. Mackinday stayed in her bedroom and heard Koppenhaver going through drawers in the kitchen. Mackinday believed Koppenhaver was looking for a knife to kill her with and in fear of her life ran out of the house and began knocking on neighbors doors to call for help.

Koppenhaver was last seen in a blue or gray Toyota Prius bearing CA plate 6MRW024. Koppenhaver is possibly headed back to San Diego.

LVMPD 514 (Rev. 8/00) x AUTOMATED

ID responded to hospital to take photos of Mackinday's injuries. Mackinday suffered a blow out fracture of her left eye, and was admitted to Sunrise hospital pending results of CT scan and internal injuries.   DV Detectives responded to the scene and hospital to take over the investigation.

5. LVMPD Event 140808-0494. On Friday August 8th 2014 at approx 0530 hours officers made contact with victim Corey Thomas at Sunrise hospital while investigating a Battery DV w/SBH under event 140808-0491.

Thomas stated that he was in bed with his girlfriend Christine Mackinday at her residence at 3496 Pueblo Way when suspect Jonathan Koppenhaver entered the room, jumped on top of him and began punching him in the face approximately 15 times. Thomas stated Koppenhaver grabbed him and put him in a choke hold almost making him go unconscious. Thomas managed to get out of the choke hold and stated Koppenhaver pinned him down and began punching him in the face again. Koppenhaver threatened to have his friends kill Thomas if he told anyone and he then let him leave the residence.

Thomas went to his job in at Spring Mountain and Valley View and called police reference the incident.

Thomas was transported to Sunrise trauma for his injuries.

Thomas suffered a bone fracture and multiple contusions from being punched in the face multiple times. ID responded to hospital and the scene. DV detectives responded to take over the investigation.

6. Officer S. Schumaker P# 8743 documented his investigation on a Domestic Violence Report Form on which he indicated that Mackinday's upper and lower lip and mouth were swollen and bloody. Mackinday's nose was bleeding, and her left and right eyes were swollen and bruised. Mackinday had brusing on her back and right thigh. Photos were taken at the time of response and uploaded into LVMPD records. Mackinday completed a voluntary statement by audio interview and Thomas completed one by dictation to a responding officer. Koppenhaver was unable to be located.

7. I Detective D. Tomaino P#8278 am a member of the LVMPD Family Crimes Detail, and I was assigned to investigate this incident. My investigation revealed that Johnathan Koppenhaver has previous charges related and unrelated to Domestic Violence in the state of Nevada. Charges include but are not limited to the following: Battery Domestic Violence, Battery w/ Substantial Bodily Harm, Battery, and Possession Stolen Firearm.

Mackinday was found to be further suffering from a lacerated liver. Mackinday was admitted for observation to determine if surgery will be necessary to repair her injury. Mackinday has extensive facial injury identified by multiple fractures and breaks. Thomas's injuries included a broken orbital and fractures throughout his face as well. Both victims injuries are still be evaluated and the final diagnosis for both is forthcoming.

Mackinday was further found to have sexually assaulted by Koppenhaver. A Sexual Assault Interview was conducted by Sexual Assault Detective J. LaFreniere P#7570. Detective LaFreniere's interview is in brief as follows:

On 8-8-14, Detective J. Lafreniere P# 7570, with the Sexual Assault Unit of the Las Vegas Metropolitan Police Department (LVMPD) responded to Sunrise Hospital and conducted an interview with Christine (Christy) Mackinday DOB 5-9-91. Christy had been admitted to Sunrise Hospital and was assigned room 6216 in the Trauma Department. Christy has substantial visible injuries to her face, including swelling and lacerations. Due to the injuries Christy's speech was not always clear and Detective Lafreniere occasionally had to repeat Christy's answers to her, so Christy could verify her account and to assure clarity. The following is a paraphrased version of the interview. The interview was recorded and will be transcribed for full, specific content. Christy relayed the following:

She is 23 years old and she resides at 3496 Pueblo Way Las Vegas, NV 89169. She has been an "on-again, off-again" dating relationship with Jonathan (Jon) Koppenhaver for the past 15 months. Currently they are in a dating relationship and she identified Koppenhaver as her "boyfriend".

Koppenhaver does not live with Mackinday, though he does have a key to her residence, and has spent the night at her house. Koppenhaver is a professional fighter, owns a clothing company called "Alpha Male Clothing Company", and he resides in San Diego, CA. Koppenhaver has a phone number of (619) 818-9050. He drives a 2010 Toyota Prius with California license plates and a bumper sticker which reads "I heart Christy Mack".

On 8-8-14 Mackinday was at home, asleep in her bed, in the master bedroom. Mackinday was wearing a grey tank top, and grey and white shorts. Mackinday's friend Corey Thomas was also at Mackinday's home and sleeping in the same bed as Mackinday. Mackinday described she and Thomas are currently in a "non-sexual relationship", though have had sex in the past.

At approximately 1:30-2 am she woke up to her dogs barking (2 pit bulls that were also sleeping in her bed) and Koppenhaver walking into her room (Koppenhaver was wearing camo Tom's, dark grey cargo shots, and a white shirt which read "Alpha Male Shit Clothing Company") and turning on the light. Koppenhaver then attacked Thomas while he was lying in the bed and Koppenhaver began punching Thomas in the face. Mackinday asked Koppenhaver to stop and Koppenhaver continued to punch Thomas, **(1 Count) Battery w/ Substantial Bodily Harm.** While Koppenhaver was beating Thomas, Mackinday dialed 911 from her cell phone, � and hid the phone from Koppenhaver. Mackinday did not say anything to the operator and she left the phone with an open line. Mackinday explained Koppenhaver choked Thomas by placing Thomas in a "rear naked choke". Mackinday described this as Koppenhaver placing his arm around Thomas's throat and grabbing his arm with his other hand to "get a good grasp". The fighting continued for approximately 10 minutes and Koppenhaver eventually released Thomas from the choke hold **(1 Count) Strangulation.** Thomas was bleeding "profusely" from his face and Koppenhaver had Thomas's blood on his shirt. Koppenhaver told Thomas to leave and told Thomas that he would kill him if he reported this and Koppenhaver went to jail. Koppenhaver said he would give his friends all of Thomas's information and his friends would find Thomas and kill him if anything happened to Koppenhaver.

After Thomas left, Koppenhaver turned his hitting to Mackinday. Mackinday said Koppenhaver first began hitting her when she was in the area between her bedroom and bathroom. Mackinday could not remember where Koppenhaver hit her first. Initially Mackinday said she did not think she lost consciousness but she later explained that due to not being able to remember all details, she may have lost consciousness **(Count 1) Battery w/ Substantial Bodily Harm DV-Related.**

Koppenhaver then took Mackinday's clothes off of her and he forced her to take a shower (in the bathroom attached to her master bedroom). While she was in the shower Koppenhaver continued to yell at her (she could not recall what he was yelling), **(1 Count) Kidnapping DV-Related.**

The next thing Mackinday recalled was being on the bathroom floor, naked, and Koppenhaver continued to hit her in the face. Mackinday recalled Koppenhaver punched and kicked her left leg while she was in the fetal position on the ground. Mackinday further recalled being on "all fours" by the shower and Koppenhaver kicked her in the ribs. Mackinday described Koppenhaver broke several of her teeth while punching her, **(Count 2) Battery w/ Substantial Bodily Harm DV- Related.**

Mackinday remembers Koppenhaver going through her Instagram and Twitter accounts (@ChristyMack) and everytime Koppenhaver found something he did not like, he would hit her in the face with both, open and closed fists. To look though Mackinday's accounts, Koppenhaver used Mackinday's cellular phone (white Galaxy S4 with a white "Mophie" case).

While Mackinday was lying on the ground in the bathroom Koppenhaver told her "that's my pussy and I'm gonna take it back now". Koppenhaver then licked his hand and put it on her vagina, **(1 Count) Open and Gross Lewdness DV-Related.** Mackinday denied that Koppenhaver penetrated her vagina at all and denied any other sexual contact. Koppenhaver did tell her that he was going to rape her but he "could not get hard" and he was mad about it. Mackinday did not see if Koppenhaver exposed his penis. Mackinday consented to a sexual assault examinations. Due to her condition Mackindays could not be removed from Sunrise to have the examination and Detective Lafreniere requested that SANE Nurse Jeri Dermanelion respond to Sunrise Hospital to conduct the examination.

8. Mackinday further identified Koppenhaver with a dull kitchen knife that had a broken handle. She stated Koppenhaver had held it to her head and threatened her with it. Mackinday escaped when Koppenhaver told her he needed to finish the job and went to the kitchen looking for a sharper knife. Mackinday heard Koppenhaver down in the kitchen going through drawers, with metal objects clanging on the counter. When Mackinday heard the noise, she went out the bedroom door to the back yard and escaped, **(1 Count) Attempted Murder DV-Related.**

9. Due to the above information disclosed by victims Christine Mackinday and Corey Thomas to Officers S. Schumaker, M. Truax, and Detective J. Lafreniere the following is understood: Koppenhaver then attacked Thomas while he was lying in the bed and Koppenhaver began punching Thomas in the face. Mackinday asked Koppenhaver to stop and Koppenhaver continued to punch Thomas, **(1 Count) Battery w/ Substantial Bodily Harm.** While Koppenhaver was beating Thomas, Mackinday dialed 911 from her cell phone, (818) 233-5190, and

hid the phone from Koppenhaver. Mackinday did not say anything to the operator and she left the phone with an open line. Mackinday explained Koppenhaver choked Thomas by placing Thomas in a "rear naked choke". Mackinday described this as Koppenhaver placing his arm around Thomas's throat and grabbing his arm with his other hand to "get a good grasp". The fighting continued for approximately 10 minutes and Koppenhaver eventually released Thomas from the choke hold **(1 Count) Strangulation.**

After Thomas left, Koppenhaver turned his hitting to Mackinday. Mackinday said Koppenhaver first began hitting her when she was in the area between her bedroom and bathroom. Mackinday could not remember where Koppenhaver hit her first. Initially Mackinday said she did not think she lost consciousness but she later explained that due to not being able to remember all details, she may have lost consciousness **(Count 1) Battery w/ Substantial Bodily Harm DV-Related.**

Koppenhaver then took Mackinday's clothes off of her and he forced her to take a shower (in the bathroom attached to her master bedroom). While she was in the shower Koppenhaver continued to yell at her (she could not recall what he was yelling), **(1 Count) Kidnapping DV-Related.**

The next thing Mackinday recalled was being on the bathroom floor, naked, and Koppenhaver continued to hit her in the face. Mackinday recalled Koppenhaver punched and kicked her left leg while she was in the fetal position on the ground. Mackinday further recalled being on "all fours" by the shower and Koppenhaver kicked her in the ribs. Mackinday described Koppenhaver broke several of her teeth while punching her, **(Count 2) Battery w/ Substantial Bodily Harm DV- Related.**

While Mackinday was lying on the ground in the bathroom Koppenhaver told her "that's my pussy and I'm gonna take it back now". Koppenhaver then licked his hand and put it on her vagina, **(1 Count) Open and Gross Lewdness DV-Related.** Mackinday denied that Koppenhaver penetrated her vagina at all and denied any other sexual contact. Koppenhaver did tell her that he was going to rape her but he "could not get hard" and he was mad about it.

Mackinday further identified Koppenhaver with a dull kitchen knife that had a broken handle. She stated Koppenhaver had held it to her head and threatened her with it. Mackinday escaped when Koppenhaver told her he needed to finish the job and went to the kitchen looking for a sharper knife. Mackinday heard Koppenhaver down in the kitchen going through drawers, with metal objects clanging on the counter. When Mackinday heard the noise, she went out the bedroom door to the back yard and escaped, **(1 Count) Attempted Murder DV-Related.**

Wherefore, declarant prays that a Warrant of Arrest be issued for suspect JOHNATHAN KOPPENHAVER on charge(s) of (1 COUNT) BATTERY W/ SUBSTANTIAL BODILY HARM, (1 COUNT) STRANGULATION, (2 COUNTS) BATTERY W/ SUBSTANTIAL BODILY HARM DV-RELATED, (1 COUNT) KIDNAPPING DV-RELATED, 1 COUNT) OPEN AND GROSS LEWDNESS DV-RELATED, AND (1 COUNT) ATTEMPTED MURDER DV-RELATED.

I declare under penalty of perjury under the law of the State of Nevada that the foregoing is true and correct.

Executed on this 9th day of AUGUST, 2014.

DECLARANT: _____

WITNESS: _____   DATE: _____
                                                              8-9-14

LVMPD 314 (Rev. 8/00) § AUTOMATED

In addition, Ms. Mack also posted graphic images of her injuries on Twitter from her hospital bed. She was having difficulty speaking at the time because of the severity of her injuries—so this was her forum of choice. She explained that she wanted to set the record straight via social media to avoid being labeled unfairly in the press.

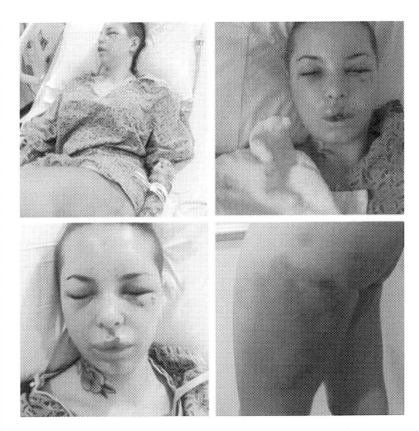

Christy Mack posted these photos of her injuries from her hospital bed, reportedly suffered at the hands of her estranged boyfriend Jonathan "War Machine" Koppenhaver. She stated in the post: "I thought I was going to die."

War Machine went on the run subsequent to these attacks, evading a warrant for his arrest until August 15. As reported in Hensley (2014):

> *Jonathan Koppenhaver, 32, was booked into the Clark County Detention Center Saturday morning on several charges stemming from the alleged attack of Christy Mack, 23, an adult film star he dated until they broke up in May.*
>
> *He waived extradition from California, where he was captured on Aug. 15 while hiding at a Simi Valley hotel room for one week on the lam as police tracked him on battery charges.*
>
> *It's believed Koppenhaver viciously beat Mack and stripped her naked on Aug. 8 at her Las Vegas home. He threatened her with a knife and then beat her new boyfriend, too.*

War Machine, as his chosen name implies, has had a long history of violent behavior, both inside and outside of the ring. This includes time in jail for assault, as reported in Thomas (2012):

After earning a year-long jail sentence in a San Diego jail on felony assault charges as well as three years of probation in 2010, the former UFC welterweight used the experience and a 2011 release to begin forging a new, more responsible path in life...

In an attempt to settle a two-year litigation battle over another previous physical altercation in Las Vegas, Nev. gone wrong, Koppenhaver accepted a plea deal with the local district attorney: in exchange for no jail time and a restitution fine of $60,000, he'd plead guilty to the charges of assault.

However, the judge in that case made it clear that she did not think War Machine was reformed. She put her concerns about his anabolic steroid abuse on the record. War Machine, however, felt that he had been treated unfairly by the court. He made that clear in a blunt statement to the press (Thomas, 2012):

"I signed [the plea deal]. I went in front of the judge," Koppenhaver told Ariel Helwani Wednesday on The MMA Hour. *"She just looked at me. She was like, 'Look at you! You look like you're going to pop! I think you're on steroids!' She started going after me. She goes, 'You know what? I'm not going to honor this plea agreement. You need to go to jail!' I was shocked. I didn't even think it was possible. I thought there was no chance of that happening. It hurt a lot. I think it was irresponsible on her part because I just did a year. I changed my ways. I don't know what she was doing. She's crazy."*

In a post to his Twitter account, War Machine was even more explicit with his disapproval of the judge, stating (Holland, 2012):

Fuck the motherfucking system! Fuck the bullshit! Vacation time, back to jail in 2 weeks! Cant stop me, all you can do is delay the inevitable. War Machine will always be back! Oh ya the judge looked at me and said she can tell Im on steroids and that thats prolly why I got in so many fights and am angry... lol Bitch.

Ultimately, War Machine's verbal behavior and history of violence paint a clear picture that is consistent with anabolic steroid abuse. They also serve as an explicit cautionary tale for those in public safety who can often be found worshipping and seeking to emulate so-called "Ultimate Fighters," and other aggressive sports figures.

This case further provides graphic evidence of what abuse looks like in terms of the consequences to oneself and one's intimates. The inflated ego (complimenting the inflated physique), the violent public threats, the failure to take responsibility, and the entitlement go hand in hand with irrational delusions. Like the notion that breaking into someone's home and sexually assaulting them can be described as merely a marriage proposal gone bad.

CHAPTER 2

Terms and Definitions

In order to understand illegal anabolic steroid use, it is necessary to familiarize readers with the related language and laws. In this section, major terms are defined and explained through the perspective of the forensic (legal) and medical communities. These explanations can be used to promote understanding, communication, and accountability—as claims of ignorance are the first line of defense when law enforcement or the judiciary are asked to account for any respective inaction or complicity.[1]

2.1 ADDICTION

The National Institute on Drug Addiction defines *addiction* as a "chronic, relapsing disease, characterized by compulsive drug seeking and abuse, and by long-lasting chemical changes in the brain" (NIDA, 2006, p. 8). It may also be defined as the continued and compulsive repetition of any behavior or activity despite adverse consequences. It is important to understand that anabolic steroid abuse is a form of addiction that can cause users to leave rational thought behind and engage in all manner of related criminal enterprise—as with any drug addiction.

2.2 ANABOLIC EFFECT

The promotion of tissue growth along with the reduction of body fat, specifically with respect to increased muscle development and definition, is referred to as an *anabolic effect* (DEA, 2004; NIDA, 2006). This is the desired result of steroid abuse. That is to say, the rapid build up of

---

[1]In 2007, a steroid abuse scandal occurred within the NYPD. It will be discussed more in Chapter 7. All of the police officers involved (at least 39 members of the NYPD) had prescriptions from the same clinic, filled by the same doctor, for *hypogonadism*. As reported in Gardiner (2007): "The primary line of defense for those [police employees] with positive steroid tests may be to claim ignorance." A police union source, speaking on the condition of anonymity, tries to make that case. "These guys relied on a doctor's advice," the source says. "He did tests, blood work. What they hell do you expect them to know about it? They're just cops." Given that law enforcement officers have no problem understanding parallel issues with oxycontin abuse, this excuse rings hollow.

muscle tissue and the reduction of body fat are the intended physical effects for steroid abusers. There are other undesirable physical and mental health consequences, and those will be discussed in later sections.

2.3 ANABOLIC STEROIDS

As explained by the DEA's Office of Diversion Control (DEA, 2004): "Anabolic steroids are synthetically produced variants of the naturally occurring male hormone testosterone. The full name for this class of drugs is **androgenic** (promoting masculine characteristics) **anabolic** (tissue building) **steroids** (the class of drugs)... The common street (slang) names for anabolic steroids include arnolds, gym candy, pumpers, roids, stackers, weight trainers, and juice." Consequently, those who abuse anabolic steroids are often referred to as "juicers."

2.4 ANABOLIC STEROID ABUSE

Anabolic steroid abuse is a phrase used to describe administering anabolic steroids for illegal or nonprescription purposes. This includes performance enhancement and image enhancement. It is often characterized by using high doses and different types of steroids to achieve a specific or synergistic outcome. Anabolic steroid abuse can lead to, and is often evidence of, addiction.

2.5 PIEDs

PIEDs is an acronym for "performance- and image-enhancing drugs." This is a generic reference to any drug that can be used to rapidly increase ability, increase muscle definition, or decrease body fat. This includes anabolic steroids, human growth hormone, and an array of drugs like Clenbuterol (a.k.a., Clen) and Adderall.[2] As explained by the Australian Crime Commission (ACC, 2014):

> The performance and image enhancing drugs (PIEDs) trade is a highly profitable and increasing international market.

---

[2]*Clen* and *Adderall* prescriptions are very popular among celebrities and reality television stars as a means for rapid weight loss—however, they also associated with irrational behavior. Adderall is an amphetamine, while Clenbuterol is a beta 2 agonist. Both are appetite suppressants and promote fat loss with muscle retention. In high doses, both can also cause mania, delusions, and psychosis.

Illicit performance and image enhancing drug use has typically been associated with body builders and elite athletes and, in a law enforcement context, with steroid abuse by members of outlaw motor cycle gangs and other criminal groups.

Current intelligence suggests the use of performance and image enhancing drugs is widespread and includes a broad range of people from a variety of occupations. Users include members of specific occupations (such as, but not limited to, security providers, military and law enforcement personnel), amateur and semi-professional sportspeople as well as elite athletes. These drugs are also used by general members of the community seeking to enhance their physique or lose weight.

Performance and image enhancing drugs are readily available through social networks of like-minded individuals, individuals within legitimate businesses such as gyms, sporting clubs and fitness centres, forged prescriptions, compliant doctors and pharmacists, thefts from medical sources (such as hospitals), the veterinary industry and via internet sales. The internet plays an important role not only in sourcing PIEDs but also in providing information on their use.

Research indicates that the drastic escalation in the use of PIEDs by members of the general public over the past decade is related to increased overall obesity (Graham et al., 2009). This in combination with an almost pathological interest in obtaining a physically "perfect" physique (high muscle definition and low body fat) as constantly portrayed in popular media.

2.6 SCHEDULE III CONTROLLED SUBSTANCES

In response to nationwide problems with addiction and abuse, the Anabolic Steroid Control Act of 1990 classified anabolic steroids as Schedule III Controlled Substances. This sets it on the same legal footing as drugs like ketamine and prescription-strength gamma hydroxybutyric acid (GHB). The Anabolic Steroid Control Act of 2004 "amended this law to increase the number of AASs that were included and make it easier to add additional drugs" (Humphrey et al., 2008).

Subsequent to a steroid abuse scandal that involved criminal investigations into hundreds of public safety employees (e.g., police officers, firefighters, sheriff's deputies and correctional officers), the Attorney General's Office for the State of New Jersey prepared a report to explain that anabolic steroids are listed as Schedule III

Controlled Substances with related criminal penalties for abuse (AGSSG, 2011, p. 5):[3]

> Pursuant to the Anabolic Steroids Control Act of 1990, anabolic steroids were added to Schedule III of the Controlled Substances Act and are defined as "any drug or hormonal substance chemically and pharmacologically related to testosterone (other than estrogens, progestins, corticosteroids and dehydroepiandrosterone)." 21 U.S.C. § 802(41)(A). The statute then lists 49 separate chemical substances that are considered anabolic steroids. U.S.C. § 802(41)(A)(i)−(xlix). Under federal law, possession or sale of anabolic steroids without a valid prescription is illegal and simple possession of illegally obtained steroids is subject to a maximum penalty of a year in prison and a minimum $1,000 fine for a first offense. 21 U.S.C. § 844(a). A first offense for trafficking steroids is punishable by up to 5 years in federal prison and a fine of up to $250,000 For second offenses, the prison time and fine can double.

As further explained in DEA (2014), the following applies to Schedule III Controlled Substances:

> Drugs and other substances that are considered controlled substances under the Controlled Substances Act (CSA) are divided into five schedules. An updated and complete list of the schedules is published annually in Title 21 Code of Federal Regulations (C.F.R.) §§ 1308.11 through 1308.15.
>
> Substances are placed in their respective schedules based on whether they have a currently accepted medical use in treatment in the United States, their relative abuse potential, and likelihood of causing dependence when abused. Some examples of the drugs in each schedule are listed...
>
> Substances in this schedule have a potential for abuse less than substances in Schedules I or II and abuse may lead to moderate or low physical dependence or high psychological dependence.
>
> Examples of Schedule III narcotics include: combination products containing less than 15 milligrams of hydrocodone per dosage unit (Vicodin®), products containing not more than 90 milligrams of codeine per dosage unit (Tylenol with Codeine®), and buprenorphine (Suboxone®).
>
> Examples of Schedule IIIN non-narcotics include: benzphetamine (Didrex®), phendimetrazine, ketamine, and anabolic steroids such as Depo®-Testosterone.

It is important to understand that the lists of controlled substances provided by the DEA are intended to be guidelines only, and that the failure of a substance to be listed is not necessarily related to whether

[3]The New Jersey law enforcement steroid abuse scandal that broke throughout 2010, and the fallout, will be discussed in Chapter 7.

use, possession, or distribution is a crime. To make this point clear, related criminal statutes usually include generic language to create legal prohibitions against the possession and distribution of unnamed anabolic steroids (i.e., "any anabolic steroid or any salt, ester, or isomer of a drug or substance described or listed in this statute, if that salt, ester, or isomer promotes muscle growth").

A booklet that provides a more complete list of controlled substances can be found on the Drug Enforcement Administration's website at: http://www.deadiversion.usdoj.gov/schedules/orangebook/orangebook.pdf. This document is routinely updated and readers are encouraged to reference the most current version.

In addition, local state laws often provide a list of specific Schedule III controlled substances, which includes opiates and steroids (e.g., *California Penal Code*, Health and Safety Code Section 11053–11058; *Official Code of Georgia,* Section 16-13-27 "Schedule III"; and *Florida Penal Code,* Section 893.03 "Standards and Schedules").

In any case, some of the anabolic steroids specifically listed in current legislation include, but are not limited to:[4]

- 4-Dihydrotestosterone (a.k.a., Anabolex, Andractim, Pesomax, Stanolone)
- 4-Hydroxy-19-nortestosteron
- 4-Hydroxynortestosteron
- Androisoxazole
- Androstenediol
- Androsterone
- Bolandiol
- Bolasterone
- Boldenone (a.k.a., Equipoise, Parenabol, Vebonol, dehydrotestosterone)
- Chlorotestosterone
- Clostebol (a.k.a., Alfa-Trofodermin, Clostene, 4-chlorotestosterone)
- Dehydrochlormethyltestosterone (a.k.a., Oral-Turinabol)
- Delta1-dihydrotestosterone
- Depo-Testosterone

[4]This is an incomplete list of examples. There are variations of these drugs, under different names, that are just as illegal to possess and distribute without a prescription.

- Desoxymethyltestosterone
- Dihydrotestosterone
- Drostanolone
- Ethylestrenol
- Fluoxymesterone (a.k.a., Anadroid-F, Halotestin, Ora-Testryl)
- Formebolone
- Formyldienolone
- Mesterolone (a.k.a., Androviron, Proviron, Testiwop)
- Methandienone (a.k.a., Danabol)
- Methandranone
- Methandriol
- Methandrostenolone
- Methasterone
- Methenolone
- Methyltestosterone (a.k.a., Android, Oreton, Testred, Virilon)
- Mibolerone
- Nandrolone
- Norethandrolone
- Nortestosterone
- Oxandrolone
- Oxymesterone
- Oxymetholone
- Quinbalone
- Stanolone
- Stanozolol
- Testolactone (a.k.a., Android-T, Androlan, Depotest, Delatestryl)
- Testosterone[5]
- Trenbolone.

Additionally, those abusing anabolic steroids can often be found ingesting animal steroids as an alternative. In fact, there are plenty of websites that advocate and facilitate this practice. Animal steroids commonly used by those looking to increase muscle mass include the following (some of these are called out above because of their inclusion in specific anabolic steroid legislation):

---

[5]*Testosterone* is not an anabolic steroid. Increased testosterone is the intended result of anabolic steroid abuse. However, it is listed in drug legislation because it is just as illegal to possess in non-prescription contexts and is often found in relation with anabolic steroids.

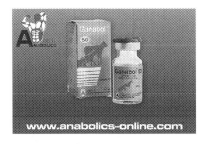

Taken from the website anabolics-online.com, Ganabol is advertised as available for human consumption, despite being clearly labeled for use by large farm animals. The distributor is listed as a foreign pharmaceutical company: V. M. Labaratorios of Colombia.

- *Equipoise* (a.k.a., Boldenone Undecyclenate, Ganabol, Equigan, and Ultragan): Used for horses.
- *Finaplix* (a.k.a., Trenbelone): Used for cattle.
- *Winstrol* (a.k.a., Stonozolol): Used for dogs and cats.

For example, if someone is found to have Boldenone in their system, it is important to understand that this is a drug specifically prescribed for use in horses and cattle. In the United States, it may only be legally prescribed by a veterinarian. It may not be legally prescribed to, or consumed by, a human. Consequently, a person testing hot for Boldenone in the United States is breaking the law in one form or another—either by receiving and possessing Boldenone illegally via the Internet; by stealing it from a veterinarian; or by allowing a veterinarian or someone that works with animals to provide Boldenone to them illegally. In other words, if someone tests hot for Boldenone, then this should initiate an immediate criminal investigation that doesn't end until the supplier is identified. This should lead to other users and more arrests until the entire supply and distribution chain are rolled up.

2.7 STACKING

The use of multiple steroids at the same time is referred to as *stacking* (Trenton and Currier, 2005). With respect to steroid abusers, this practice "may be done to produce a synergistic effect by exploiting different androgen receptors or merely to achieve a higher overall dose" (p. 574). "Stacking" steroids is typically not a feature in any legitimate course of medical treatment (AGSSG, 2011). In other words, if a urinalysis reveals the presence of multiple steroids in a subject's system, then this is strong evidence suggestive of abuse and related illegal activity.

2.8 SUPPLEMENTS

Dietary *Supplements* are legal products (pills, powders, and liquids) that are advertised as containing vitamins, minerals, proteins, herbs, or some combination of these that are alleged to promote building muscle mass or fat burning. In the United States, the makers of dietary supplements can legally offer vague assurances of promoting health and well-being. However, ordering them from overseas is another matter.

It is well known that the production of supplements outside of the United States is unregulated. This is often why they are purchased, as opposed to simply using supplements that are legally available within our borders. Those seeking the benefits of illegal anabolic steroids do this to avoid the appearance of purchasing and importing a Schedule III controlled substance, but generally know full well what they are doing.

As a result, claims by abusers that they have ingested anabolic steroids unwittingly in the form of a supplement will generally ring hollow. First, the only supplements that might have this effect are from outside of the United States. Purchasing expensive supplements outside of the country is not necessary for the lawful user. Second, an investigation will likely yield not only long-term use but also the overt procurement of illegal anabolic steroids by other means. The onus is on the investigator in such cases to identify all of the sources of anabolic steroids in the suspect's life, and not just take the abuser's word that they somehow became confused when ordering supplements in bulk from China.

2.9 T/E RATIO

The *T/E ratio* is the proportion of **T**estosterone (T) to **E**pitestosterone (E) detected in the urine. The human body creates testosterone and its precursors naturally. Therefore, when testing for anabolic steroid abuse, it is necessary to distinguish between naturally produced testosterone and that which is the result of taking drugs or supplements. On average, a normal T/E ratio is 1, with some variation possible on either side.

Taking anabolic steroids and related supplements suppresses natural steroid production. In abusers, the concentration of testosterone in the urine is expected to be higher than normal owing to direct ingestion of the drug. However, epitestosterone levels will remain suppressed. Therefore, a urinalysis that reveals lowered epitestosterone levels in concert with abnormally high testosterone levels is indicative of anabolic steroid use.

A T/E ratio of greater than 6 is considered evidence of anabolic steroid abuse. Consequently, drug testing labs will often use that number as evidence of a presumptive positive when initially screening urine for the presence of anabolic steroids. A presumptively positive result initiates a more sensitive test to confirm the true T/E ratio. With chronic abusers, this number will be significantly higher than 6, easily rising up into the 30s and beyond. That is because, as explained in Swanson et al., 1991 (p. 20): "when individuals begin self dosing... the typical usage under these and related circumstances is 10 to 100 times greater than a proper medical dosage."

The authors have found this to be true in both their research and casework. For example, consider *Kramer et al. v. City of Jersey City et al.* (2011).

In a 2011 Appellate Court ruling, the court upheld a police department's right to test officers and remove them from active duty based on the T/E ratios. The complaining officers argued that their rights had been violated by the department's testing policy, and the Federal appeals court disagreed. Taken from the original decision in *Kramer et al. v. City of Jersey City et al.* (2011):[6]

> In particular, the Officers object to the District Court's observation that "[g]enerally, high steroid levels [are] linked to aggressive behavior," (App. 6), from which it inferred that drug testing, modified duty, and suspensions were reasonable measures taken to ensure that Jersey City police officers using steroids were neither dangerous nor unfit for duty. However, the Officers do not deny the uncontroversial proposition that high steroid levels have been linked to aggressive behavior. See generally Nat'l Inst. on Drug Abuse, Nat'l Insts. of Health, Pub. No. 06-3721, Research Report: Anabolic Steroid Abuse 5 (2006), available at http://drugabuse.gov/PDF/RRSteroids.pdf. We hold that the District Court did not err by taking judicial notice of this relationship...

---

[6] This court decision stems from the New Jersey police steroid scandal of 2010–2011, which will be discussed in a later section.

Accepting plaintiffs' allegations as true and drawing all inferences in their favor, see Torisky v. Schweiker, *446 F.3d 438, 442 (3d Cir. 2006), we agree with the District Court that the Officers' allegations cannot establish a viola-tion of their constitutional rights.*

Police officers "are members of quasi-military organizations, called upon for duty at all times, armed at almost all times, and exercising the most awesome and dangerous power that a democratic state possesses with respect to its residents—the power to use lawful force to arrest and detain them." Policemen's Benevolent Ass'n of N.J., Local 318 v. Washington Twp. *(Gloucester County), 850 F.2d 133, 141 (3d Cir. 1988). "The need in a democratic society for public confidence, respect and approbation of the public officials on whom the state confers that awesome power" is compelling. Id.; see* Nat'l Treasury Employees Union v. Von Raab, *489 U.S. 656, 677 (1989). At the same time, police departments require "officers who are physically and mentally capable of working in dangerous and highly stressful positions, sometimes over long peri-ods of time."* Fraternal Order of Police, *Lodge No. 5 v. City of Phila., 812 F.2d 105, 114 (3d Cir. 1987). Thus, "police officers have little reasonable expectation that . . . medical information will not be requested."*

. . .

See Von Raab, *489 U.S. at 671 ("[T]he public should not bear the risk that employees who may suffer from impaired perception and judgment will be promoted to positions where they may need to employ deadly force.").*

To be clear, the court held in this opinion that there is a relation-ship between steroids and increased aggression that is largely indisput-able; that police officers need to be of sound mind to do their jobs, especially given that they carry firearms and have the power to deprive people of their lives and liberty; and that elevated T/E ratios are a valid and reasonable mechanism for assessing officer mental fit-ness for duty in this regard. Consequently, police departments can compel steroid testing and then use those results to bench and investi-gate officers. They can also share that information with other police departments.

As further discussed in Mueller (2011):

The opinion by the 3rd Circuit Court of Appeals in Philadelphia amounts to a victory for Chief Tom Comey, who contended throughout the lengthy legal fight he had an obligation to ensure the officers did not pose a risk to the public given the link between steroids and increased aggression.

More significantly, the ruling puts the appeals court's imprimatur on an issue that has not been widely addressed at the federal level. While the courts have repeatedly upheld law enforcement policies that test for illegal drugs, they have not tackled the use of testosterone and other steroids obtained with a prescription, leaving chiefs in a legal gray area.

In the Jersey City case, the officers obtained prescriptions from a doctor who, authorities say, faked diagnoses in many cases to accommodate clients' desires to get bigger and stronger. Some of the drugs were then sent by mail from a Brooklyn pharmacy investigators determined was little more than an illegal steroid mill.

University of Texas professor John Hoberman—who tracks steroid use in law enforcement and who has written widely about the rise of hormone replacement therapy, along with its abuses—called the ruling a "groundbreaking" opinion that should make it easier for police chiefs to take action against officers who bulk up under the guise of hormone therapy.

"In the past, police officials have tended to back off of strict enforcement, because they simply did not know how to handle medical claims by officers," Hoberman said. "This judge has refused to allow the medical claim to dictate the outcome of the case, and that is a breakthrough for the anti-steroid rules that many departments have not enforced in a consistent way."

The appellate opinion, released Tuesday, affirms a lower court decision dismissing the claims brought by officers Nicholas Kramer, Brian McGovern and Patrick Fay. They were among more than 40 Jersey City officers who obtained anabolic steroids or human growth hormone from Lowen's Pharmacy in Brooklyn, court records show.

The drugs had been prescribed by Jersey City physician Joseph Colao, the subject of a series of stories in The Star-Ledger last year.

Comey, who was tipped to the steroid use by a New York City internal affairs captain, ordered his officers to undergo tests and put them on modified duty pending the results. Officers who had elevated levels of testosterone—a hallmark of steroid use—remained on desk duty until those levels returned to a normal range.

This 2011 decision is a powerful tool for law enforcement administrators and supervisors concerned about the legality of testing police employees for steroid abuse. It should also serve to provide a clear rationale for such testing, and any subsequent departmental response in the interest of public safety. Conversely, departments not testing for elevated T/E ratios when a reasonable suspicion of steroid abuse exists could be found negligent in later civil actions brought in relation to officer misconduct.

2.10 CONCLUSION

In order to have an informed discussion about the illegal use of anabolic steroids, it is necessary for criminal justice professionals to understand what they are, how they are identified, and that they are actually illegal. Currently, many of those in law enforcement and the judiciary claim ignorance on these subjects. Still more act out of what can only be described as apathy, by failing to facilitate the necessary legal consequences for those found in possession of, or distributing, controlled substances. This sends the wrong message to the criminal justice community, and to the public in general, about law enforcement tolerance for criminal behavior. This to say nothing of undermining police integrity.

Criminal justice professionals have an obligation to know the law, uphold the law, and maintain their professional integrity by exemplifying lawful behavior. Otherwise, their sworn oaths and codes of ethical conduct mean little or nothing. Those violating the law, and those turning a blind eye, are undeserving of the trust that has been afforded to them by the public.

On that issue, the court has made it clear that public safety agencies and employees cannot hide behind the Health Insurance Portability and Accountability Act (HIPAA) in order to protect themselves from the stain of scandal. Instead, they have an obligation to ensure that all employees are fit for duty and to protect the public from any potential related harms. This includes testing for all illegal and/or mind-altering drugs, and making sure that those results are both acted upon and shared with current and potential future employers.

Case Example
Officer Albert Smith, Phoenix Police Department

In 2007, Officer Albert Smith of the Phoenix Police Department in Arizona spoke to the press regarding his use of illegal anabolic steroids. He had tested positive and been suspended as part of an investigation into area police officers and firefighters. Confusion around the issue, and clear flouting of the law by many of those involved, was reported in KPHO (2007):

> *"There's tons of guys out there, tons of guys, on the fire department, on the police department, that are using," said Albert Smith, a Phoenix police officer suspended after testing positive for steroids on the job.*
> *"My honest opinion? I don't believe they should be illegal," Smith said. "I think it's a personal decision. I'm not hurting anybody."*
> *Doctors prescribe steroids to treat inflammatory diseases and abusers use them to bulk up, but research shows that abusing steroids can hurt the user's body. Steroids can cause heart attacks, high cholesterol and aggressive behavior.*
> *CBS 5's original investigation turned up more than a dozen officers and firefighters from departments across the Valley who faced allegations of domestic violence, rage and suicidal threats.*
> *Former detective Trinka Porotta, now a drug consultant in Mesa, said departments have an obligation to protect their employees and the public. "They have to be blind not to see it," Porotta said.*
> *But Commander Kim Humphrey said identifying steroid abusers can be difficult. "It's not as easy as testing them and coming back with a*

positive test," Humphrey said. "It seems like that's how it should work, but it doesn't."

Humphrey said some steroid tests have shown false positives, while other positive results were never passed on to the department. "We're aware of at least one, only because we had the individual on another investigation, and then he told us," Humphrey said.

Smith fought to keep his job and won, but most officers tied to steroids have resigned rather than face termination.

Robert Welch, a Phoenix firefighter and police reserve officer, was one of them. Cut from the police department, Welch is still on the job as a firefighter. "If I walked into a room and I saw a police officer and a fireman injecting steroids and they both didn't have a script for them, the police officer would get fired; the fireman would get wellness. That sends a conflicting message," the police recruit instructor said.[7]

"You're talking about apples and oranges here. We have a different set of rules," said Assistant Fire Chief Mark Angle. "Police officers enforce the law. We do not."

Angle said the Phoenix Fire Department only tests new recruits for steroids. Veteran firefighters are tested only if they act out on the job. "We want to make sure that when any of our folks get on a truck and they go out there and they provide service to the community, that we're not sending out damaged goods," Angle said.

In early October of 2013, Patrol Officer Smith was arrested for domestic violence charges related to crimes committed against his wife. As reported in Hoey (2013):

Phoenix police officer Albert Smith's mugshot subsequent to his arrest for domestic violence.

[7]As will be discussed in the following section, the problem is that many prescriptions for anabolic steroids are obtained via deception or unlawful means—just as with other addictive and highly abused drugs like Oxycodone.

According to the Maricopa County Sheriff's Office, Albert Smith got into a fight with his wife, Donna, on the night of Thursday, Oct. 10. Deputies say Smith punched his wife in the face, causing a bruise on her forehead.

Smith also reportedly suffered some injuries in the fight. Both Smith and wife were arrested in the incident.

The argument happened at the couple's Mesa home, after Donna had reportedly thrown a birthday party for her husband earlier that night.

According to court documents, Donna says her husband got upset during the party, and the pair continued the argument later at home. That's when Donna says Albert Smith held her down and punched her several times in the face.

Donna admitted to deputies that she bit her husband's fingers, believing it was the only way she could defend herself. She later secretly called 911.

As a result of this arrest, Officer Smith was suspended from active duty pending an internal investigation.

Officer Smith also had an apparent history of excessive force complaints, as claimed in a lawsuit filed against him just prior to his first suspension for illegal steroid use (*Vera v. Smith et al.*, 2005):

Plaintiff sues the City of Phoenix Police Department and one of its officers, Albert Smith. Plaintiff alleges that Officer Smith, during an arrest, punched Plaintiff behind his head with a gun, slammed Plaintiff's face on the sidewalk, put his knee in Plaintiff's head, and then kicked Plaintiff. Other unidentified officers arrived and joined Smith in kicking Plaintiff. They did not stop until they heard over their radios that civilians were watching. Plaintiff also alleges that the officers were deliberately indifferent to his medical needs. He suffered various physical injuries, including fractured ribs and a bump on his head. For relief, he requests an award of 3.5 million dollars and an order for medical treatment. These allegations adequately state a claim against Defendant Smith, and the Court will require him to answer the Complaint.

To be clear, Officer Albert Smith of the Phoenix Police Department had a history of excessive force. He also had a history of illegal steroid use that was known by his department (a.k.a., possession). He further admitted that use of illegal steroids by him and other area police and firefighters was commonplace. He publicly argued that the use of steroids should be legalized because they had no harmful side effects, and then later got arrested for charges of domestic violence related to an attack on his wife. Moreover, he publicly stated to the press that he had no intention of following department policy regarding anabolic steroid use, despite acknowledging that it was a crime, because he felt it shouldn't be.

This means that he acknowledged the law he was sworn to uphold, and then let it be known that he would not be following it. Yet he was retained by his department until his arrest for a crime that is often found linked to the abuse of anabolic steroids. And there was no attempt to source the origin of the illegal drugs he was using, or otherwise roll up the supply chain on this case.

The current legal status of Officer Smith's criminal charges, as of this writing, is unclear.

Case Example
Detective Christopher Kitcho, Atlanta Police Department

On August 19, 2014, Detective Christopher Kitcho of the Atlanta Police Department resigned from the Narcotics Unit rather than face termination. This after he failed a departmental drug test. However, the 34-year-old Kitcho did not quit while he was ahead, and eventually he suffered legal consequences.

Mugshot of former Atlanta Police Department Detective Christopher Kitcho.

On August 29, just 10 days later, Kitcho was arrested, as reported by Cook (2014):

> ...[former Detective Kitcho] was arrested on charges of possession of cocaine, marijuana and a controlled substance and possession of a weapon while in the commission of a crime.

> *Campos said Atlanta police officers found drugs, anabolic steroids and a rifle when they searched Kitcho's north Atlanta apartment after he was arrested in DeKalb County for impersonating an officer. Kitcho allegedly showed his APD badge to DeKalb officers questioning him about an alcohol-related citation. Consequently, Atlanta officers went to his apartment to search for any other APD equipment he had not returned.*

So Kitcho apparently got stressed because of his forced resignation and the related shame of a failed drug test, and then went on a bit of a drinking bender. While intoxicated, he apparently forgot that he was no longer allowed to act under color of authority. He subsequently tried to get out of trouble the way that one does while doing bad things on the job—by flashing the tin. And it backfired.

It is important to understand that anabolic steroids are often used in conjunction with other illegal drugs to manage undesirable side effects (discussed later in this text). This includes depression and anxiety, which can be masked by alcohol and stimulant abuse. These coping mechanisms are often found in full bloom subsequent to high-stress incidents, such as court dates, failed drugs tests, resignations, or terminations.

Despite official claims from the Atlanta Police Department that the current chief "will not tolerate illegal drug use among officers or any employee of the police department, and (he) is prepared to take the appropriate disciplinary actions for anyone who violates those policies" (Cook, 2014), there is no evidence of any investigation into the suppliers or dealers of the anabolic steroids discovered in the Kitcho case. The failure to question public safety officers about their suppliers with respect to illegal anabolic steroids is a common investigative omission and suggests that those running the case typically do not want to know.

CHAPTER 3

The Problem: Anabolic Steroids and Law Enforcement Culture

The anabolic steroid abuse problem within law enforcement is straight-forward. Police culture embraces images of aggression and masculinity, serving up both institutional and social rewards for those that conform (Sweitzer, 2004; Crowder and Turvey, 2013). Denying this overwhelming reality is not reasonable. Anabolic steroids help provide an easy path to those short-term rewards. However, these rewards are temporary, high risk, and illegal. Additionally, as with any form of illegal drug use, it doesn't occur in a vacuum. Anabolic steroid abuse requires committing any number of crimes and direct association with other criminals—including those who deal other illegal drugs (Humphrey et al., 2008).

This brings us to the crux of the problem. Those in public safety have a need to maintain the perception of a heroic image; to make sure that the badge remains untarnished. They cannot be seen to break the law and abuse mind-altering drugs while also maintaining the necessary integrity, fitness for duty, and public trust required to do their job (e.g., make arrests without incident, make life-and-death decisions, drive a vehicle, sign affidavits, and give sworn testimony). Consequently, very few in the criminal justice system want to admit that there is an anabolic steroid abuse problem, even when the physical and behavioral manifestations of steroid addiction are front and center.[1]

3.1 LAW ENFORCEMENT CULTURE

It is helpful to review the research on law enforcement culture, in order to understand that there are certain traits and values shared by those in law enforcement and related public service careers (e.g., firefighters).[2]

---

[1] The authors have observed that police officers and their families deny steroid abuse as part of the cycle of addiction; public safety agencies deny it so that they don't have to take any corrective or punitive action that might bring further liability; and the courts deny it, hoping to protect prior convictions from the stain of law enforcement misconduct.

[2] This section is adapted from original research in Turvey (2013).

Waddington (1999) describes law enforcement as being a canteen or clannish subculture, explaining (p. 287): "The core referents of 'police sub-culture' are clear enough: its sense of mission; the desire for action and excitement, especially the glorification of violence; an Us/Them division of the social world with in-group isolation and solidarity on the one hand, and racist components on the other; its authoritarian conservatism; and its suspicion and cynicism, especially towards the law and legal procedures."

This is reinforced by the research presented in Terrill et al. (2003), that occupational pressure, anxiety, and strain "produce two defining out-comes of police culture—isolation and group loyalty" (p. 1006). Paoline (2004) goes on to report that law enforcement (p. 207) "attitudes, values, and norms include a distrust and suspiciousness of citizens and a pre-scription to assess people and situations in terms of their potential threat (i.e., maintaining the edge), a lay-low or cover-your-ass orientation to police work that would discourage the initiation of contacts with citizens and supervisors, a strong emphasis on the law enforcement elements of the police role, a we-versus-they attitude toward citizens, and the norm of loyalty to the peer group."

Wolfe and Picquero (2011) agree, providing that (p. 334) "[p]olicing is characterized by a close-knit subculture because the 'unique demands that are placed on police officers, such as the threat of danger as well as scrutiny by the public, generate a tightly woven environment conducive to the development of feelings of loyalty'" (Skolnick, 2005, p. 302).

These posters are often found hanging in the walls of law enforcement agencies and offices, to serve as a reminder of what might await them on the street and to be prepared for it.

Along these same lines, Benson (2001) reports that machismo, militarism, racism, and a code of silence are primary elements of law enforcement culture, reporting (pp. 685–686): "Instead of acting upon the extensive evidence of differences between men and women police—and recruiting and promoting more women—police departments nationwide are bastions of ... 'open sex discrimination and sexual harassment' and negative attitudes toward female officers."

This is expounded by research presented in Garcia (2005), which demonstrates that law enforcement culture emphasizes crime fighting, force, and masculinity while at the same time devaluing its internal social service functions that are associated with femininity. See also Benson (2001), reporting that (pp. 682–683):

> Machismo, or what some have called hypermasculinity, is the value system that celebrates male physical strength, aggression, violence, competition, and dominance. It denigrates the lack of these qualities as weak, female behavior. ...
>
> The practical results of this police machismo are that male officers get themselves involved in hostile confrontations with the public, use of excessive force, shootings, drug dealing, and apparently, as we see now in the Rampart scandal, framing of suspects through deceit and lies.

This issue was also explored in research presented by Harris (2000), which revealed that men in law enforcement culture experience intense pressure not to be perceived as feminine or homosexual, and that violence and aggression are the means used to assert and maintain a strong male identity.

What this means is that law enforcement culture rewards both men and women for conforming with exaggerated images of masculinity. It pushes officers to overcompensate with strength and aggression in order to prove the absence of sentiment and weakness (Crowder and Turvey, 2013; Sweitzer, 2004). And all of this before the issue of anabolic steroids has even been raised.

3.2 FITNESS FOR DUTY

Fitness for duty refers to the ability to safely and effectively perform one's job-related responsibilities with integrity. This means the absence of physical, psychological, and character impediments. Fitness for duty in a law enforcement or public safety context is important because the consequences of failure, or inability, are high. When public safety officers are not fit for duty, people can be harmed if not killed. Those at risk can include the unfit officer, fellow officers, other public safety personnel, victims, suspects, and any unfortunate bystanders.

The legal responsibilities related to police officer fitness for duty are explained in Fischler et al. (2011, p. 72):

Police employers have a legal duty to ensure that police officers under their command are mentally and emotionally fit to perform their duties, and failure to do so can result in significant civil liability to the employer and serious consequences. Occasionally, a law enforcement officer's behavior raises concerns that the officer may be unstable, a physical danger to self and to others, or ineffective in discharging responsibilities. Such behavior may occur on or off duty and may include excessive force, domestic violence, lack of alertness, substance abuse, or other observable counterproductive behaviors.

Red flags, or indicators, of an officer's lack of fitness include (adapted from Fischler et al., 2011):

– Making false statements to supervisors, in reports, or in testimony
– Observed symptoms of psychological distress (e.g., excessive crying, irritability, or paranoia)
– Making threats against others
– Suicidal threats or attempts
– Admission to any facility for mental health issues
– Irrational behavior
– Delusional behavior
– Consistent failure to complete official duties despite corrective action
– Consistent failure to comply with basic departmental rules and directives despite corrective action
– Disclosure of a significant mental health issue or a mental health diagnosis or the use of psychotropic medication
– Suspicion of drug abuse (prescription or street drugs)
– Multiple citizen complaints
– Involvement in an accident
– Incurring a physical injury
– 911 call to the officer's home
– An arrest for any crime
– A conviction for any felony, or any misdemeanor related to integrity, vice, or violence.

As explained in Fischler et al. (2011), the existence of these red flags should initiate an officer evaluation (p. 72): "When such behavior occurs, and it is reasonably suspected to be attributable, at least in part, to an underlying psychological impairment or condition, a Fitness-For-Duty Evaluation (FFDE) is often necessary to assess the nature of the psychological problem and its impact on job functioning." Failure to acknowledge these indicators and conduct an FFDE would be considered negligence on the part of the department, and compound liability with respect to leaving an unfit employee on the street, perhaps even carrying a firearm.

As explained by the International Association of Chiefs of Police, anabolic steroid abuse leads directly to a lack of fitness (Humphrey et al., 2008):

> Agencies have a duty and a right to maintain fit officers and to protect the public from impaired officers. They must exercise reasonable means at their disposal to ensure that officers are fit. Both national and local standards regarding the use of AASs support the idea that officers abusing such substances could be at risk for impairment and could even be involved in criminal activity related to the use of these substances.

Consequently, any FFDE must include a drug test. Testing for controlled substances will either rule out drug use as an underlying cause, or it will identify drugs in the officer's system that may not have been disclosed prior. This drug test must also include a panel for anabolic steroids, or it is selectively excluding an entire set of illegal drugs that are commonly abused by public safety personnel.

3.3 THE PEACE OFFICER'S MISSION

Law enforcement is ostensibly trained to keep the peace. That is to say, they are intended to be deployed to enforce the law and maintain public order. This is to protect citizenry and property. In all situations, they are meant to respond in a way that maximizes public safety by de-escalating violence when they can. Their mission, ultimately, is to respond with only the force necessary to resolve crises. Despite how the policing mission may be distorted by some line officers and administrators, they are not intended to escalate the violence of any given situation.

Anabolic steroid abuse, as will be demonstrated, works against this mission in every way. First, it creates the presentation of physically aggressive imagery (i.e., a large and muscular officer); aggression begets an aggressive response. Second, it increases an officer's aggressive tendencies in general (see generally Humphrey et al., 2008). And finally, it gives those who use them a physique that they want to put to use. In other words, use of anabolic steroids provides the motive and means for hyperaggressive behavior, while employment in law enforcement and public safety provides the opportunity.[3] This is an undesirable combination, rife with legal liability.

Consequently, anabolic steroid abuse, in terms of both psychological impact and underlying officer motivations, works against the peacekeeping mission of law enforcement. Those who use them are not putting their role as a peace officer first. Rather, they are more concerned about image and ego. Worse, they are creating the circumstances for a physically violent confrontation to become a likelihood as opposed to a last resort.[4]

3.4 CRIMINAL PROCUREMENT

In the United States, anabolic steroids cannot be lawfully procured for performance or image enhancement. This means that any public safety officer abusing anabolic steroids must be doing so by criminal means. These include prescriptions under false pretenses; procurement from a foreign country; or procurement through an illegal drug dealer (AGSSG, 2011; Sweitzer, 2004; Wilairat, 2005).

If an anabolic steroid abuser is receiving their drugs with a doctor's prescription, they are generally doing so through deceptive practices. This means that they do not have a proper doctor–patient relationship, and/or they are getting prescribed via a roid mill. These and related issues will be discussed more thoroughly in the next chapter.

It is common for abusers to procure anabolic steroids from foreign countries. This can be accomplished by ordering them from an Internet website run by a foreign laboratory or distributor. This can also be accomplished by virtue of travel to a foreign country where anabolic

---

[3]Sweitzer (2004) goes further, arguing (p. 213): "in response to the escalating levels of violence [in the war on drugs], the police got ever more violent. The exaggerated level of violence and threat naturally engendered an exaggerated masculinity, and an overstated muscularity... cops on steroids are simply the natural evolution of a conscious decision by the federal government to promote military authoritarianism in drug enforcement, and the implementation of military technologies."

[4]These themes will be explored more thoroughly in Chapter 6.

steroid sales are unregulated, such as Mexico, China, or Thailand. Regardless, bringing anabolic steroids into the United States is a federal crime—whether delivered through the mail or secreted through customs at the border.

It is also common for anabolic steroid abusers to buy their drugs of choice from drug dealers. These dealers may be other public safety officers; fellow abusers that they met at a local gym; or a dealer that sells an array of illegal substances. Regardless, it is a crime. The officer is committing a crime when they make the buy just as the dealer is committing a crime when they make the sale. It is no different than the illegal purchase of cocaine, oxycontin, or meth.

When buying from a drug dealer, they must consort with, and even identify themselves to, a known criminal in order to get their drugs. This puts them in physical danger, as well as leaving them vulnerable to threats and extortion in exchange for law enforcement access and consideration (Hladky, 2012). Again, this is no different than the dangers associated with an addiction to any other illegal drug.

3.5 CONCLUSION

Law enforcement has a professional obligation to public safety that includes employing and deploying only those officers that are fit for duty. As is demonstrated and explained throughout this manual, it is not possible to use anabolic steroids and also maintain psychological or character-related fitness for duty. However, because of related performance- and image-enhancing benefits, in combination with ignorance of the law, anabolic steroid abuse is tolerated by some public safety agencies and many in the legal community. This short-sighted approach, which amounts to the burying of heads in the sand, ensures that harm will be caused and that legal liability will be incurred.

Case Example
Thomas Kantzos, David Vo, and Craig Hermans, Arlington Police Department, TX

In early June of 2013, David Vo and Thomas Kantzos, both of the Arlington, TX, Police Department, were arrested as the result of a joint FBI and Texas Ranger investigation into an illegal anabolic steroid ring.

Officer Kantzos, a 17-year veteran of the department, was arrested and charged with fraud for his part (CBS, 2013a). He was not only a user, but a conduit facilitating the flow of illegal anabolic steroids into the department. He bonded out to await trial.

Officer Vo, on the job for only 3 years and working in the Gang Unit, was arrested for illegally buying and distributing anabolic steroids in connection with Kantzos—his apparent mentor. He also bonded out. Soon after being released, Officer Vo committed suicide; his body was found in an open field with a handgun nearby (CBS, 2013a).

Also placed on administrative leave at the same time was fellow Arlington police officer, and confessed anabolic steroid abuser, Craig Hermans. CBS (2013b) reports: "On Officer Craig Hermans' original application he admits to using steroids... Hermans blamed his steroid use on being skinny and having low self-esteem. He claimed after six doses he stopped using and never did it again."

Officer Thomas Kantzos' official departmental photo, alongside of his subsequent arrest mugshot in the Arlington Police Department steroid scandal of 2012. He was sentenced to a year in prison.

The following is an excerpt from the June 12, 2013 affidavit of FBI Special Agent Nils A. Hubert with respect to his investigation of this case:

4. In January 2013, an individual was arrested for distributing anabolic steroids and he agreed to be a cooperating witness (CW). During interviews in which I participated, the CW admitted to routinely using and distributing anabolic steroids and human growth

hormones (HGH) during the last 13 years. For the last 5 or 6 years, the CW has routinely provided anabolic steroids and HGH directly to THOMAS KANTZOS, whom the CW knows to be a City of Arlington Police Officer. On at least one occasion, the CW delivered approximately 20 HGH kits to KANTZOS while KANTZOS was on duty, wearing an Arlington Police Officer uniform, and driving an Arlington Police Department marked patrol car. According to the records of the Texas Commission on Law Enforcement Officer Standards and Education (TCLEOSE), KANTZOS has been an Arlington Police Officer since October 1995.

5. A consent search of the CW's cellular telephones revealed the content of text messages between the CW and telephone number 817-296-XXXX, which was identified in the CW's telephone directory as being associated with "Thomas." Those text messages occurred between approximately January 31, 2012 and January 16, 2013. Telephone records reflect that KANTZOS is the subscriber for telephone number 817-296-XXXX and has been the subscriber since before January 2010.

6. A review of text messages between CW and KANTZOS obtained from the CW's cellular telephone, and information obtained during interviews I conducted with the CW, reveal that KANTZOS was familiar with the types, dosages, uses, and prices of various forms of anabolic steroids. On multiple occasions, KANTZOS solicited anabolic steroids from the CW for himself and other individuals, including friends and colleagues in the Arlington Police Department. He often collected money from the other individuals before he obtained the steroids from the CW, but on some occasions he fronted the money for the purchases. KANTZOS was aware the CW utilized the mail service to obtain and distribute anabolic steroids.

7. Based on their conversations, the CW knew KANTZOS took most of the anabolic steroids and HGH he obtained from the CW and distributed them to other Arlington Police Officers. Additionally, KANTZOS put the CW into contact with two other named Arlington Police Officers so they could obtain anabolic steroids directly from the CW.

8. A review of text messages in the CW's cellular telephone revealed that on August 2, 2012, KANTZOS texted "What kind of deca you got" and the CW responded "Qv only got couple till next order hits." KANTZOS responded "How much … Gotta a guy wanting a bottle." According to the CW, "deca" refers to the anabolic steroid Deca Durabolin, and "Qv" refers to the "Quality Vet" brand of testosterone.

9. A review of text messages in the CW's cellular telephone revealed that on September 19, 2012, KANTZOS texted "Got a couple orders" and the CW responded "Ok." KANTZOS replied with the text message "One test... 100 Winnie 100 Anavar." According to the CW, "test" refers to testosterone and Anavar and "Winnie," or Winstrol, are steroids.

10. A review of text messages in the CW's cellular telephone revealed that on January 9, 2013, KANTZOS texted the CW the message "Boy from work wants a test and a dec ... " The CW responded "Ok" and KANTZOS texted "$190 for both?" According to the CW, "dec" refers to the anabolic steroid Deca Durabolin.

11. On April 12, 2013, the CW conducted a consensually recorded meeting with KANTZOS. During their conversation, KANTZOS used his cellular telephone to text and call Officer A, who KANTZOS indicated was an Arlington Police Officer who used anabolic steroids. KANTZOS asked the CW if he recognized the names of two people who had supplied anabolic steroids to Officer A prior to their arrests. KANTZOS also asked what anabolic steroids the CW possessed when arrested and how the CW obtained them. KANTZOS explained he was trying to determine if there were any connections between Officer A's steroid supplier and the CW KANTZOS told the CW "All our sources dried up."

12. Also during the recorded meeting on that date, KANTZOS asked the CW "Remember about two years ago I had a guy who bought 20 bottles from you?" Near the conclusion of the meeting, KANTZOS told the CW, "You'll be back in business" and "I got like five guys that are fucking 'jonesin'" (wanting to obtain steroids).

13. According to the CW, KANTZOS has provided the CW with law enforcement sensitive information that KANTZOS obtained from law enforcement databases. Access to those databases is restricted to authorized law enforcement personnel only. In each instance, the CW asked KANTZOS to query a name or a license plate for the CW's personal use.

14. The Texas Department of Public Safety confirmed that KANTZOS is authorized to access law enforcement information obtained through the Texas Crime Information Center (TCIC) and the National Crime Information Center (NCIC). In order to qualify for that access, KANTZOS received specialized training on the authorized uses of the information, as well as the potential penalties for the misuse of such information.

Personal use of such information including releasing information to members of the general public is not authorized and violates Arlington Police Department policy. He can access TCIC and NCIC information utilizing the Texas Law Enforcement Telecommunication System (TLETS). TLETS is a secure computer network utilized only by law enforcement personnel. KANTZOS can access TLETS using a unique user identification and password specifically assigned to him. Patrol cars used by the Arlington Police Department are equipped with computers that allow patrol officers to use TLETS.

15. The CW stated that on a Thursday in November or December 2011, the CW saw a suspicious pickup truck parked down the street from the CW's house and a familiar looking man appeared to be looking at a laptop computer in the driver's seat. The CW asked KANTZOS to "run" the truck's license plate, because the CW planned to deliver anabolic steroids to a named Arlington Police Officer later that day and the CW was concerned about the possibility of police surveillance of his activities. KANTZOS told the CW that the vehicle was owned by Individual B, whom the CW had previously met and knew to be a police officer on a drug task force. TLETS records reflect that on Thursday, December 29, 2011, KANTZOS conducted a "Stolen Vehicle Investigative Inquiry" for the license plate of a pickup truck registered to Individual B, who is a law enforcement officer.

16. Based on the information provided by KANTZOS, the CW visually inspected his vehicle and discovered a tracking device attached to it. The CW immediately began "laying low" for 3 or 4 weeks, during which time the CW and KANTZOS talked about the tracking device and the police surveillance of the CW. A review of text messages on the CW's cellular telephone revealed that on February 16, 2012, KANTZOS texted the CW the message "Still laying low?" The CW replied with the text message "Yeah got new way of doing you still need?" KANTZOS responded "Let me ask ... But (name redacted) was asking bout it too."

17. A review of text messages on the CW's cellular telephone revealed that on October 29, 2012, at approximately 11:06 a.m., the CW texted KANTZOS and asked if he would "run a plate" which the CW provided. KANTZOS responded with the message "Let me ask someone at work. In off today." At approximately 11:50 a.m. that same day, KANTZOS sent the CW a text message with an embedded photograph of a computer screen displaying the registration information for the same license plate number that the CW had requested. According to information from the computer display, the registration query was conducted at 11:48 a.m. on October 29, 2012. A check of the TLETS records revealed that on October 29, 2012, at 11:48 a.m., Individual C from the Arlington Police Department

conducted a "Vehicle Registration Inquiry" of the same license plate as the CW provided to KANTZOS.

18. A review of text messages on the CW's cellular telephone revealed that on December 1, 2012, at approximately 10:27 a.m., the CW texted KANTZOS the message "What up" and KANTZOS responded with the text message "Who you want me to run." The CW replied with the name, age, and date of birth for Individual D. KANTZOS then sent the CW two embedded photographs of a computer screen displaying the driver's license information of Individual D. A check of TLETS records revealed that on December 1, 2012, at 10:30 a.m., KANTZOS of the Arlington Police Department conducted a "Driver License Inquiry" regarding Individual D.

19. A review of text messages on the CW's cellular telephone revealed that on April 24, 2013 at approximately 1:46 p.m., the CW texted KANTZOS the message "Can you run a plate for me" and KANTZOS responded with the text message "Prolly call a bud to." At approximately 2:15 p.m. that same day, the CW texted KANTZOS a license plate number. KANTZOS responded with two messages that included the vehicle registrant's name and city of residence, as well as the name of the person who insured the vehicle. A check of TLETS records revealed that on April 24, 2013, at 2:16 p.m., Individual E from the Arlington Police Department conducted a "Combination License Plate Registration Inquiry with Stolen Vehicle Inquiry" for the license plate number the CW provided to KANTZOS.

20. On June 1, 2013, at approximately 11:19 a.m., the CW texted KANTZOS the message "Hey I just pulled up at my old connections house can you run a plate on alexis here." The CW's text message also included a license plate number. KANTZOS responded to the text "Give me a few ... I'm not in my car." At approximately 11:57 a.m., KANTZOS sent the CW a text message containing the name and city of residence of Individual F. According to the results of a vehicle registration query investigators conducted on that same license plate on April 23, 2013, the information KANTZOS provided to the CW was accurate.

21. THOMAS S. KANTZOS knew that the CW was distributing drugs in violation of state and federal law when the CW asked KANTZOS to run queries on law enforcement databases including TCIC and/or NCIC, which are contained within protected computers, and are intended for law enforcement purposes only. Instead, KANTZOS knew he was providing restricted information to someone who was not an authorized recipient, and who was also a known drug dealer, in order to aid and abet that drug dealer's illegal steroid distribution activities.

Confronted with this information, Kantzos admitted to his role in aiding and abetting the illegal steroid dealer that sold to members of his department (CBS, 2014):

> *Former officer Thomas Kantzos, 45, pled guilty to one count of Exceeding Authorized Access to a Protected Computer. Prosecutors say Kantzos improperly used a police computer to help tip off his steroids dealer.*
>
> *Kantzos admitted to using a computer system reserved for law enforcement at the request of the suspected drug dealer to warn him about police surveillance. Kantzos used the computer in his patrol car, while on duty, to "run" the license plate number provided to him by the suspected drug dealer, even though he knew it was illegal to do so.*

Thomas Kantzos, fired by the department subsequent to his arrest, was eventually sentenced to a year and a day in jail.

Officer Craig Hermans, however, resigned rather than face further investigation by his department; a public records search indicates that no criminal charges were filed against him (Schrock, 2013).[5]

As a result of this scandal, the Arlington Police Department sought and received funds to start conducting random drug tests on all of its members. Arlington Police Chief Will D. Johnson warned (CBS, 2013a): "If I find out that they're doing illegal drugs, they will be terminated… Criminal misconduct by our employees is intolerable as it damages the trust and confidence of those we serve. We will always aggressively pursue the arrest and prosecution of any employee engaged in this sort of behavior". This is a worthwhile sentiment, but allowing officers to resign in lieu of criminal charges sends entirely the wrong message.

Case Example
Dep. Darrion Holiwell, King County Sheriff's Office, WA

On June 19, 2014, Darrion Holiwell of the King County Sheriff's Office was arrested. He was a 19-year veteran of the department, as well as being a member of Tac-30 (the SWAT team); serving as the chief firearms instructor at the county gun range; and running a private firearms-training business on the side called Praetor Defense. He was charged with promoting prostitution, theft, and both dealing and abusing anabolic steroids (Kruse, 2014).

---

[5]It is important to understand that justice is negotiated by lawyers and the courts. It is not a strict matter of fact or law. Therefore, outcomes vary. This is no excuse for the failure to conduct an investigation, however, as those results provide the mechanism for any subsequent plea deals.

A month later, in July, he was fired by Sheriff John Urquhart, who stated (Burton, 2014): "Darrion Holiwell violated his oath, the trust of his fellow deputies, and the trust of the citizens of King County... He does not deserve to be a police officer."

Darrion Holiwell of the King County Sheriff's Officer prior to his arrest in June 2014.

In August, Holiwell pled guilty to multiple charges, as reported in Sullivan (2014):

> *A King County judge didn't mince words after former King County sheriff's deputy Darrion Keith Holiwell admitted in court Monday that he helped his wife work as a prostitute, stole from the department and delivered drugs.*
>
> *"It is difficult for the court to comprehend how somebody who swore to protect the public and to uphold the law could engage in these serious crimes," Superior Court Judge Bruce Heller said. "You are a disgrace to your profession by engaging in these actions."*
>
> *...The Sheriff's Office began investigating Holiwell in April, after his estranged wife went to his previous wife to find out if the other woman had endured domestic violence while with Holiwell, authorities said. The former wife mentioned the conversation to a friend who is a sheriff's employee and the employee notified supervisors.*

Darrion Holiwell was undone not by his lack of fidelity to fellow officers, to his sworn oaths, or to the citizens he had sworn to protect and serve. He was undone by his own ego, his reckless criminal behavior, and his lack of fidelity in personal relationships, as reported in KOMO Staff (2014; see also facts and evidence referenced in *Washington v. Darrion K. Holiwell*, 2014):

> *Holiwell's transgressions first came to light during divorce proceedings with his third wife, Alicia Holiwell. According to the charging*

documents, Alicia had been physically abused by Holiwell, though she did not report the incidents, and she contacted his previous wife, Dana Smith, to see if there was a pattern. Smith was reportedly so over-whelmed by what Alicia told her, she contacted a friend who works for the sheriff's office. That friend notified her supervisor, and an investigation began.

Alicia told sheriff's office detectives her marriage with Holiwell had been troubled, in part because of her affairs. According to the charging documents, Holiwell eventually accused her of being a sex addict and said, "If you are going to have sex, you might as well get paid for it."

Holiwell reportedly told Alicia her extra income would help with the family's financial burdens and could help him start a new security business. Holiwell already had one side business offering firearms training and accessories.

Holiwell and Alicia separated in May 2013—supposedly temporarily to work on their marriage—and Alicia got her own condo. According to the charging documents, she started her escort business shortly after.

Alicia told detectives Holiwell provided her advice on how to run the business, and in the beginning she would text him her clients' IDs and inform him when she was with a client as a security measure.

Once the business got going, Alicia was making $2,000 a weekend, and Holiwell would collect approximately 80 percent of the profits, according to the charging documents.

During this time, Holiwell reportedly supplied Alicia with human growth hormone to lose weight and marijuana and "molly," a form of Ecstasy, to help with her escort appointments.

According to the charging documents, this arrangement ended when Holiwell started dating Alicia's 20-year-old friend, violating the terms of their open relationship. Alicia got angry and filed for divorce.

Following the interviews with Alicia, detectives served search warrants at Holiwell's home and the Sheriff's Office firing range.

Further details regarding the specific criminal charges, and the ongoing investigation into other members of the department, are reported in Sullivan (2014; see also facts and evidence referenced in *Washington v. Darrion K. Holiwell*, 2014):

Holiwell's theft conviction stems from his trading of 67 cases of ammunition worth more than $15,000 to two gun shops in exchange for credit to obtain tactical gear and firearms parts.

Sheriff John Urquhart, in announcing Holiwell's arrest in June, said the probe also uncovered evidence that Holiwell, chief of the department's Ravensdale shooting range, sold about 19,000 pounds of brass from expended shell casings to three gun shops in exchange for some cash, but mostly for merchandise used by the SWAT team, including gun sights and barrels.

"Basically, tricking out their weapons," Urquhart said in June. "Lots of stuff, to the tune of about between $45,000 and $50,000 between 2007 and currently. Essentially what it was was a slush fund for the SWAT team off the books, at least off our books."

Holiwell's drug conviction stems from his possession and sales of drugs, including steroids... Investigators seized nearly 100 bottles of illegal steroids in his home. The man told investigators that he had sold Holiwell steroids since soon after meeting him in 2012, and also sold him cocaine, Cialis and the club drug Molly, charging papers said. The man said he lived rent-free in exchange for drugs.

Kevin McDaniel, a Seattle police officer, is also named in charging documents as purchasing testosterone from Holiwell several times, most recently in early April 2014. McDaniel is under investigation by the Police Department's Office of Professional Accountability. Seattle Police Officers' Guild President Ron Smith said McDaniel had been on administrative leave, but has since returned to work...

Two other deputies have been placed on paid leave as the investigation into Holiwell's actions continues. One, a woman who worked in the major-crimes unit, is suspected of tipping Holiwell to the investigation. No details were provided on why the other deputy, who works at the shooting range, is on leave.

Darrion Holiwell in court, pleading guilty to multiple felonies, in August of 2014.

Darrion Holiwell was ultimately sentenced to 366 days in prison. He plead guilty to second-degree promotion of prostitution; domestic violence; first-degree theft; and to the violation of a drug law. This plea included three felony charges. As a result, Holiwell will not be allowed to own or possess any firearms for the rest of his life, in accordance with local and federal law governing convicted felons and those convicted of offenses related to domestic violence.

There can be no question regarding the role that law enforcement and SWAT culture played in the case of Darrion Holiwell. However, it also demonstrates how anabolic steroid abuse, for some, can be an indication of other personal problems. Someone that needs steroids to look strong and be strong has something to prove. Using one drug to compensate for inadequacy can lead to doing others, and to other behaviors motivated by the need to relieve feelings of inadequacy (e.g., promiscuousness, controlling others sexually, and coercing others into acts of sexual degradation). This is a common nexus of behaviors and motivations found among anabolic steroid abusers.

CHAPTER 4

Legal Use: Prescriptions for Anabolic Steroids

Anabolic steroids are classified by the DEA, and the FDA, as Schedule III controlled substances. That means, unlike those classified as Schedule I, they actually enjoy a limited accepted medical use. Consequently, they may be possessed in quantities consistent with personal use, but only so long as the user has a valid prescription from a licensed medical professional.

Additionally, someone that is being treated with anabolic steroids will only be on them for a short period of time, and then only at therapeutic levels. If a person has been under a prescription for anabolic steroids for a period of years, or if they test positive for above-normal levels, then this is an indication of illegal use and abuse. As with other prescription drugs like Xanax and Oxycontin, addiction can occur whether or not they have what appears to be a legitimate doctor's prescription.

4.1 LEGITIMATE MEDICAL CONDITIONS

Anabolic steroids may be legitimately used in only select treatment contexts. For example, this includes a diagnosis of *hypogonadism*, which refers to abnormally low testosterone production in men; *AIDS*, because, as discussed by Wilairat (2005), those afflicted by and treating AIDS patients have "opposed banning steroid precursors because AIDS patients often suffer muscle atrophy and anabolic steroids help build back their wasted bodies" (p. 402); *cancer*, as anabolic steroids can help to suppress certain kinds of tumors as well as help to build back any related muscle loss; and *angioneurotic edema*, which is a rare genetic condition. They may also be prescribed as part of a physical therapy regimen to counteract muscle atrophy under certain extreme conditions.

As explained in AGSSG (2011), legitimate prescriptions for anabolic steroid treatment will involve multiple diagnostic assessments by a licensed physician, regular monitoring of patient testosterone levels, and numerous related follow-up exams (p. 4):[1]

> When prescribed appropriately, doctors typically incorporate regular monitoring of testosterone levels during treatment, including follow-up examinations within 3–6 months of initial prescription, prostate examination and dexa-scanning to assess bone density. These follow-up tests are rarely if ever utilized where patients are improperly using steroids. Moreover, an initial diagnosis of legitimate testosterone deficiency should be predicated on the combination of symptoms, physical exam and blood testing of hormone levels. Diagnosis should not be made simply based on blood test results that are merely indicative of traditional declines in testosterone levels as men age.
>
> The DEA has noted that abusers may take dosages of anywhere between 1 and 100 times a normal therapeutic use, take multiple steroids simultaneously (termed "stacking") and stay in steroid cycles of between 6 and 16 weeks of high dosage followed by a dormant period of low or no dosing. Because steroid abuse typically involves dosing at levels far beyond therapeutic use, can involve taking multiple steroids at one time (something that is rarely, if ever, prescribed as part of normal treatment) and may also incorporate illicit forms of steroids, the health risks are substantial.

It bears repeating that legitimate anabolic steroid treatments rarely involve the prescription of more than one steroid at a time, as this is generally not medically advisable. However steroid abusers will use multiple anabolic steroids in order to achieve synergistic effects. In plain language, this means that these drugs are much more powerful when used in combination than when used one at a time.

The narrow legitimate treatments for which an anabolic steroid can be prescribed, and the amount of diagnostic and related follow-up care that is required, make it relatively straightforward to identify someone that is engaged in illegal steroid use. For example, as explained in Humphrey et al. (2008): "an officer who states that a physician provided them for 'elbow pain' would be using them inappropriately." Also, if they claim that anabolic steroids have been prescribed to help build muscle mass and they already have plenty, then this would be another red flag.

The bottom line is that legitimate users of anabolic steroids will have a clear underlying medical condition that has been diagnosed by a medical professional, they will have a clear professional relationship

---

[1]This includes taking a complete medical history and conducting a thorough physical exam, as "Myocardial infarction (MI) and sudden cardiac death have been associated with steroid use... in the absence of significant medical histories or known risk factors" (Trenton and Currier, 2005, p. 575).

with their physician, and they will be able to produce a prescription from a licensed physician upon request. However, investigators must take care to verify the legitimacy of any physician prescriptions that they have been provided as evidence of legal compliance. Anabolic steroid abusers, especially those associated with law enforcement and public safety, know that such verifications take time and effort. If they think they can get away with it, they will phony up a prescription or seek one out from an unscrupulous medical professional (or Internet-based pharmacy) that is operating outside of the law (or outside of the United States).

Verification of a legitimate prescription means validating that the prescription has been issued by a medical professional currently licensed to practice in the state where it was issued; that the amount in possession is consistent with the amount prescribed and regular use; and that the labels on the bottles are genuine, and also consistent with the anabolic steroids that the physician prescribed.

4.2 CLINICS AND TREATMENT CENTERS

The law enforcement community is well aware that the abuse and illegal distribution of Oxycontin is associated with "pill mill"-style operations disguised as legitimate pain clinics or medical treatment centers. In these cases, one or less often two licensed physicians run multiple clinics in a region. They visit each clinic only a day or two a week (or month), and fill out prescriptions that they sell to patients with clear substance abuse problems. Once law enforcement is on to them, they close up shop and move to another county or state, rotating their activities until they are eventually caught and criminally prosecuted.

A similar type of situation has emerged to provide illegal anabolic steroids under the guise of legitimate medical care: the *roid mill*. These businesses, structured to maximize client base and sales with minimal adherence to the law, if any, are run under the auspices of being "wellness," "anti-aging," "longevity," "rejuvenation," or "steroid replacement treatment" clinics.[2] Sometimes these phony clinics are run by a

[2]Steroid Replacement Treatment or Therapy is a viable option for those with a specific diagnosis related to low natural male hormone production. However, as explained by the Mayo Clinic: "treating normal aging with testosterone therapy is not currently advisable" (Mayo Clinic, 2014a). This is because of the many potential adverse side effects.

physician or by an unlicensed medical professional. In extreme cases, as we will discuss, they might be run by a police officer that thinks they can operate illegally without fear of consequence because all of their customers are in law enforcement or public service.

In roid mills, anabolic steroids are prescribed to "patients" under the auspices of promoting general wellness, longer life, or replacing diminished testosterone.[3] The problems associated with roid mills are discussed by Brittain and Mueller (2011):

> By all accounts, the anti-aging business is booming, a trend fed by an eager public's timeless thirst for elixirs and pills to flatten bellies, increase vigor and improve sexual potency.
> And with every new patient and every new prescription, the medical establishment grows more alarmed.
> Critics say anti-aging practitioners, operating in a gray area of both medicine and the law, too often cross the line by peddling powerful and potentially dangerous substances on the basis of medically faulty diagnoses.
> "It's a total ruse," said Thomas Perls, an associate professor of medicine and geriatrics at Boston University Medical School and one of the anti-aging movement's more outspoken foes.
> "The population generally equates hormones with youth, and therefore for gullible or narcissistic individuals, it becomes an easy sell," Perls said. "Any claims that this stuff works for anti-aging is absolute nonsense. It's quackery."
> In recent years, prosecutors across the nation have charged dozens of doctors, pharmacists and clinic owners with illegally dispensing anabolic steroids and growth hormone to patients under the guise of anti-aging medicine.
> Yet critics say most physicians who flout the law continue to get away with it, the result of lax state medical boards, weak federal oversight and the secrecy inherent in the doctor–patient relationship.
> "Nobody's watching," said Alan D. Rogol, a University of Virginia professor and pediatric endocrinologist who has written extensively about the abuse of steroids and growth hormone. "Each patient sees his doctor, and his doctor has a doctor–patient relationship, and if he's diagnosed as deficient— however that's done—then a legitimate prescription is written."
> The U.S. Food and Drug Administration approves drugs for specific uses but doesn't monitor physicians or the practice of medicine. That's left to the states...
> Andropause, otherwise known as male menopause, has become the movement's hottest buzzword despite continuing debate among physicians about whether the condition really exists and, if it does, how prevalent it is.

---

[3]To be fair, some of these clinics don't bother with being so clever; they just prescribe steroids to promote muscle growth without a thought to the notion that this is an illegal practice. If they have local or area law enforcement among their "patients," then this is perhaps all the cover they think they need.

A study published in the New England Journal of Medicine *in June suggested just 2 percent of men between the ages of 40 and 80 show the constellation of symptoms consistent with andropause. To many doctors, the term is just another word for the body's natural aging process.*

Where anti-aging practitioners have gone astray, the critics say, is in stretching the definition of what it means to be hormone-deficient. A 40-year-old man might have normal levels of testosterone and growth hormone relative to other 40-year-old men, but the levels are likely to be well below those of a 20-year-old man.

To many anti-aging physicians, that's a deficiency.

Rogol, the University of Virginia professor, has another name for it: bad medicine. "It's a dangerous thing to put someone on testosterone unless you have a real diagnosis for a testosterone deficiency," he said.

Despite such criticism, sales of both growth hormone and testosterone continue to soar. Between 2005 and 2009, spending on various testosterone gels and liquids in the United States more than doubled, to just over $1 billion, according to IMS Health, a firm that provides market research to the pharmaceutical and health care industries. This year, doctors are projected to write more than 4 million prescriptions for the drug.

In the same time period, spending on growth hormone jumped 32.7 percent, to $1.3 billion, and the number of prescriptions climbed to 431,000, IMS Health found.

The explosive growth hasn't been lost on doctors. Across America, chiropractors, orthopedists, pain-management physicians, internists, plastic surgeons and gynecologists like Balzani are reinventing themselves as anti-aging specialists who hawk hormones on their websites.

It is important to understand that there is no scientific evidence to suggest that anabolic steroids increase longevity. With respect to wellness (good physical and mental health), there is actually strong evidence that this is necessarily diminished as well. As will be made clear in the following section, there is no good or desirable outcome to long-term steroid use and abuse. Only short-term gains in muscle size, muscle definition, and body fat reduction that come with a terrible price. And that price can include sudden death.

Consequently, the increase of doctors and clinics focusing on steroid-based treatment appears related primarily to the narcissism and ignorance of the general public, along with the profit motivations of unethical practitioners in the medical community.

Some in the law enforcement community have also jumped on the steroid replacement therapy bandwagon. For example, Chief Jeffrey Halstead of the Ft. Worth Police Department held a voluntary Wellness Seminar for police officers to share his views about the benefits of testosterone therapy. He encouraged his officers to look into it as a treatment for the stresses of working in law enforcement. As reported by Slater (2010):

> Halstead said he believes some of his officers may be better officers with a hormone adjustment. But is the product he's sharing safe?
>
> A police chief works long hours and has to make some tough decisions. Managing hundreds of police officers is a challenge. But recently, Halstead noticed something in his life was off. "Stress of the job, long hours and work—everything was getting pulled from both ends," he said.
>
> So the chief turned to SottoPelle Pellet Therapy to boost his testosterone levels. The therapy starts with a small incision under the skin. A pellet containing testosterone is inserted to raise levels of the hormone. Halstead said he now feels great again, and to share his success, he created a voluntary wellness program for the entire Fort Worth Police Department and invited the SottoPelle team.
>
> Among the topics at the seminar? Sex, because an increase in hormone levels increases sex drive...
>
> News 8 checked with independent sources about the product Chief Halstead is sharing with officers. Five North Texas doctors with expertise in hormones—representing five different hospitals and clinics—all agreed, first and foremost, that the Chief's testosterone level is too high.
>
> He went from 125, which experts said is too low, to nearly 1,000. On average, the doctors said levels should not exceed 400 to 500. That means Halstead has twice the testosterone they would recommend.
>
> But Dr. Gary Donovitz, who represents SottoPelle, says his team never overdoses hormones, and maintains there is extensive blood work for each patient. "We weren't jacking with his hormones like you would anabolic steroids," Donovitz said. "We're simply trying to return him and other men to where they should be when they were 30 with normal testosterone."
>
> UT Southwestern endocrinologist Dr. Richard Auchus says the chief is encouraging a socially acceptable form of narcotics. "There are a number of other psychological changes that occur, particularly when there is an abrupt rise from lowish levels to high levels," Auchus said. "Those include increased aggression, and some people become psychotic on it."
>
> Dr. Donovitz said doctors who don't like his organization's product usually haven't done the research. He says the therapy does just the opposite of what Dr. Auchus suggested. "It's going to lower their aggressiveness, because people with low testosterone levels—specifically males—are much more irritable, much more anxious," Donovitz said. He said the pellets are all-natural, plant-derived, and safe.
>
> Dr. Auchus doesn't buy that explanation. "Any time you take a man and you increase his testosterone levels, he experiences a euphoria from that," Auchus said. It's a euphoria he worries could become addictive.
>
> A specialist at Texas Health Arlington said "cocaine is also a plant; I wouldn't give that to my patients."

Baylor University Medical Center in Dallas called the SottoPelle treatment "mis-marketing and inappropriate." Even a wellness clinic that supports hormone replacement acknowledges that "men can become angry." A Texas Health Dallas doctor believes "there are red flags all over it."

So not only is this chief repeating what the medical community believes are "inappropriate" claims about a particular drug, but the doctor representing the drug company involved doesn't seem to fully understand how testosterone works. In any case, the net result is a chief of police with at least double the normal levels of testosterone openly encouraging his employees to join him. Given the red flags noted, this situation would seem to be an open invitation for all manner of liability.

4.3 PHONY SCRIPTS: RED FLAGS

The legitimacy of a prescription can be confirmed with basic inquiries made in relation to the red flags described in this section. It is not confirmed by the presence of a signed prescription (which can be faked), or by merely taking the word of a user (which can be a lie). Red flags for phony anabolic steroid prescriptions, indicating the need for further investigative action into potential criminal activity, include:

1. An individual is in possession of anabolic steroids without a valid prescription[4]
2. The alleged "patient" is not certain of, or cannot explain, the diagnosis related to their prescription
3. The user cannot produce a verifiable prescription in a reasonable time period
4. The user has prescriptions for multiple anabolic steroids, and from multiple physicians
5. The prescription produced does not match the name of the user
6. The amount of anabolic steroids in possession exceeds the prescription amount
7. The labels on the anabolic steroids in possession are not consistent with manufacturers' labels
8. The steroid prescribed is for animals, not humans (very common)
9. The prescribing physician is not licensed to practice in the state (or at all)

---

[4]This is a federal crime and indicates other related criminal activity such as procurement.

10. The prescribing physician has had their license revoked in other states
11. The prescribing physician is practicing outside of their speciality
12. The prescribing physician only accepts cash payments
13. The user was diagnosed over the Internet, without a physical exam
14. The user is receiving anabolic steroids from foreign countries (e.g., Canada, Mexico, or Thailand).[5]

Red flags are not necessarily proof of criminal activity on the part of the user, but must be investigated until their origins are understood and criminal activity has been eliminated as the source.

4.4 CONCLUSION

Anabolic steroids can be prescribed for a narrow field of legitimate medical conditions. Typically, they are prescribed one at a time, and by a single physician that is closely monitoring both dosage and side effects. These prescriptions do not result in dramatically elevated anabolic steroid levels, and they are generally not long term because of the potential for addiction and other harmful side effects.

Because of the growing performance and image enhancement market, roid mills have sprung up all over the United States and the illegal importation of anabolic steroids from foreign countries is at an all-time high. This means that what appears to be a legitimate prescription for anabolic steroids may be obtained illegally by falsifying information, by visiting a "clinic" that is operating in an unlawful fashion, or by getting what may be an unlawful prescription from an online source.

It is not difficult to determine when anabolic steroids are being prescribed or used unlawfully. It does, however, require thoughtful observation and basic inquiry in relation to the red flags discussed.

[5]In July 2014, shipping giant FedEx was indicted by the Justice Department for illegally shipping prescription medications, including anabolic steroids. These criminal charges were the result of an investigation into 9 years of shipments into the United States made from two foreign pharmacies. If convicted, FedEx could face up to 1.6 billion dollars in fines (Lobosco, 2014). In 2013, United Parcel Service (UPS) settled a similar case by paying 40 million dollars in order to avoid court and a possible conviction (NYT, 2014).

Case Example
West Palm Beach Police Department, Florida

In April 2014, Dewitt McDonald was allowed to plead guilty to "knowingly carrying a firearm during and in relation to a drug trafficking crime, in violation of Title 18, United States Code, Section 924(c)(1)(A)" (USA, 2014). While working as a police officer with the West Palm Beach Police Department, Officer McDonald had owned and operated multiple roid mills under false pretenses. As the result of a joint investigative effort by the FBI and FDA, the following facts were agreed to prior to sentencing (USA, 2014):

> According to the stipulated statement of facts filed with the court, the defendant was a police officer with the West Palm Beach Police Department. While employed as a police officer, the defendant operated two businesses: Prime Performance Wellness Centers, Inc., located in Lake Worth, and Prime Health and Rejuvenation Clinic, located in Wellington, through which he unlawfully distributed anabolic steroids and other prescription drugs. The stipulated statement of facts further states that on March 5, 2013, while on duty and carrying his Smith & Wesson MP40 pistol, the defendant made a delivery of these drugs to another officer of the West Palm Beach Police Department.

However, the problems at the West Palm Beach PD apparently run much deeper than just McDonald, who originally pled not guilty to an array of charges. As reported in Lantigua (2014):

> McDonald was fired after he failed to immediately respond to a call at Palm Beach Lakes High School in February 2013. It was the last of a series of problems he had during his last five years on the force, including 21 letters of reprimand and 73 days of suspensions.
> The charge that he had illegally bought and sold steroids while he was in uniform and armed was brought after he had been dismissed from the force.
> [His attorney, Michael] Salnick said the steroid abuse problem in the West Palm Beach police force goes beyond McDonald. "Obviously the activities of the entire West Palm Beach Police Department, in my opinion, deserve more scrutiny," Salnick said. He said that scrutiny should begin with "mandatory drug testing twice per week."

During his guilty plea, it became clear that former Officer McDonald was cooperating with Federal investigators, revealing the names of other police officers that he illegally sold anabolic steroids to through his clinics. His illegal activity also included forging prescriptions, as there was no physician associated with any of his businesses. These details are reported in McMahon (2014):

> McDonald, who reached a plea agreement with prosecutors and is cooperating with investigators, faces between five years and life in federal prison when he is sentenced July 18.

The former officer, who had a long history of misconduct, was fired from the police department in 2013. He was a police officer for 20 years and spent the last 18 years of his career with the West Palm Beach department.

He was one of several South Florida police officers who served suspensions for buying steroids from the PowerMedica pharmacy on Hillsboro Boulevard in Deerfield Beach. Federal authorities found patient records for several law enforcement officers in 2005 when agents raided and shut down the pharmacy for illegally selling steroids and human growth hormones.[6]

McDonald said little during the brief hearing Wednesday in federal court in Fort Lauderdale. "Guilty, sir," he replied when U.S. District Judge James Cohn asked how he wanted to plead to the charge...

Prosecutors said that while McDonald was still employed by the police department in 2011 and 2012, he opened two clinics in Palm Beach County: Prime Performance Wellness Centers Inc. in Lake Worth, and Prime Health and Rejuvenation Clinic in Wellington. Both businesses advertised testosterone and human growth hormone therapy, but prosecutors Jeffrey Kaplan and Paul Schwartz said he used the corporations to illegally sell anabolic steroids and other prescription drugs between September 2011 and April 2013...

Prosecutors said McDonald forged the signatures of doctors on prescriptions, altered prescriptions, illegally split larger vials into smaller ones and signed his name on pre-printed prescriptions that listed the doctors' names.

It is also worth noting that Officer McDonald was determined to be illegally selling other prescription medication out of his clinics—not just anabolic steroids. As of this writing, the investigation into his client list is reported to be ongoing.

Case Example
Sheriff Tommy Rodella and Son, Rio Arriba County, NM

On August 15, 2014, Rio Arriba County Sheriff Tommy Rodella[7] and his son were arrested for felony charges subsequent to a grand jury indictment a few days prior. Both were accused of violently attacking, and illegally

[6]In 2007, 13 officers with the West Palm Beach PD were suspended as a result of an investigation into the illegal use of steroids by members of the department. Dewitt McDonald was among them; he was suspended for 8 h. This means that the West Palm Beach PD did not arrest at least 13 officers that were determined to be involved in felony anabolic steroid possession.
[7]Tommy Rodella Sr. is married to New Mexico State Rep. Debbie Rodella (D).

detaining, a motorist while acting under color of official police authority. They were also charged with falsifying subsequent police reports to conceal their crimes. As reported by Cowperthwaite (2014):

> *The FBI arrested Rodella in front of his office shortly before 6 a.m. and arrested his son, Thomas Rodella Jr., at the family residence in La Mesilla a few minutes later, FBI Spokesman Frank Fisher said...*
>
> *A federal grand jury indicted Rodella and his son on Aug. 12, for alleged civil rights violations following a traffic stop and the arrest of Michael Tafoya on March 11, in La Mesilla.*
>
> *Rodella is charged with conspiracy to violate the civil rights of Tafoya, violating the man's civil rights, brandishing a firearm and falsifying a document. Rodella Jr. is charged with all of the same, except he is not charged with brandishing a firearm. The Rodellas were arraigned shortly before 10 a.m., Aug. 15 in Albuquerque District Court, following the arrest and pleaded not guilty to all the charges, court documents state.*

To be very clear: at the time of the attack, Tommy Rodella Sr. was the Arriba County Sheriff, and Tommy Rodella Jr. was serving in both the National Guard and as a reserve police officer.

As further reported, both were released without bail subsequent to a hearing. This despite concerns raised in court by the U.S. Attorney regarding both Tommy Sr.'s history of abuse of power, and Tommy Jr.'s history of steroid abuse (Cowperthwaite, 2014):[8]

> *During an afternoon detention hearing, Magistrate Judge Lorenzo Garcia released both, Rodella and Rodella Jr., on their own recognizance. As a condition of their releases, neither will be allowed to possess any firearms, explosives or deadly weapons...*
>
> *U.S. Attorney Tara Neda asked for Rodella to be released to a halfway house in Santa Fe County, citing alleged danger to Tafoya and his past history of abuse of power.*

---

[8] A judicial review found evidence that Rodella had engaged in both willful misconduct and false testimony about it when he was serving as a judge in 2005. As held *In Re Rodella* (2008): "The Commission investigated Judge Rodella's involvement in three separate cases that came before Judge Rodella and determined that he violated the Code of Judicial Conduct, Rules 21-100 through 21-901 NMRA, and committed willful misconduct in office. The first was a DWI case that occurred shortly after Judge Rodella was appointed to the Rio Arriba Magistrate Court in April 2005, in which Judge Rodella was found to have involved himself in a friend's case. The second was a landlord-tenant case that had its origins in the period between Judge Rodella's resignation in July 2005 and his subsequent election in November 2006. In that case, Judge Rodella was found to have promised to rule in favor of campaign supporters in future litigation. The third was a domestic violence case set to be heard by Judge Rodella in June 2007. In that case, Judge Rodella was found to have engaged in ex parte communications with a witness, telling her she did not have to respond to a subpoena."

Garcia said he found little credence in her worry because no harm had yet befallen Tafoya between the incident in March and the time of the hearing. "That's important," Garcia said. "There's no evidence (he has) been intimidated." Garcia said he looked kindly upon Rodella Jr.'s status as a member of the National Guard.

Neda said Rodella Jr. had a history of steroid use and wanted him to be on a no drugs condition for his release. Garcia said no drugs not prescribed by a doctor were already part of the standard conditions of release pending trial.

Later, all charges against Tommy Jr. were dismissed by the U.S. Attorney's office, owing to evidence of a severe medical condition. This was explained by Reed and Miller (2014):

The U.S. Attorney's Office on Wednesday filed an unopposed motion to dismiss federal charges against Thomas Rodella, Jr., son of Rio Arriba County Sheriff Tommy Rodella...

The charges in the five-count indictment stem from a March incident during which Sheriff Rodella and his son allegedly engaged in the high-speed pursuit and unreasonable seizure of a victim, Michael Tafoya.

The motion seeks dismissal of the charges against Rodella Jr. based on information indicating that he has a "medical condition that puts into doubt whether he has the cognitive ability to form the specific intent necessary to prove the charges against him beyond a reasonable doubt," according to a news release sent by the U.S. Attorney's Office.

At an afternoon press conference, lawyers confirmed Rodella Jr. had allegedly suffered a "traumatic brain injury" and PTSD after serving in the military and a deployment to Kosovo. The motion states that the U.S. Attorney's Office learned about the medical condition after the indictment was filed and after Rodella Jr. was arrested.

"You consider his medical background, his military service. You consider that he had a traumatic brain injury, and you look at the standards required to be proved for mental state, and this was never a case that should have been brought," [defense attorney Jason] Bowles said.

This defense becomes problematic, and raises fitness for duty issues, when one considers that Tommy Jr. was also serving as a reserve deputy and carrying a firearm under color of law enforcement authority during this timeframe. The response from his defense attorney essentially insults the professional and moral compass of every ethical officer on the job, as reported further in Reed and Miller (2014):

When Bowles was asked how Rodella Jr. could be a reserve deputy and not understand intent during the alleged altercation, he said, "It's two different things. The law in a special-intent crime requires the highest level of mental state. You have to specifically and willfully intend to commit a crime. That's different from doing your job on a day-to-day basis as a deputy. It's two different mental states. Those two don't equate to each other."

In other words, the defense attorney argued that serving as a law enforcement officer does not require a "high level of mental state" because it does not require decision making with intent. Therefore serving with a severe brain injury while heavily medicated is acceptable. Or something of that nature.

At Tommy Rodella Sr.'s trial, his brain-damaged son testified on his behalf to support their unified version of events. However, Tommy Jr.'s testimony in open court made the problems raised about his mental state even more concerning, as reported by Stiny (2014a):

Tommy Rodella Jr. is pictured subsequent to his testimony, wearing a shirt that says "National Guard, American Heroes."

Sheriff Rodella is charged with depriving Tafoya, 26, of his civil rights with an unconstitutional arrest following a high-speed chase that Tafoya says ended up with Rodella Jr. pulling him from his car and throwing him to the ground and the sheriff shoving his badge into Tafoya's face. The prosecution and Tafoya maintain the sheriff, in plainclothes and traveling with his son in his personal Jeep, never identified himself before shoving the badge and cursing Tafoya, but the Rodellas dispute that.

Rodella Jr., 26, demonstrated to the jury in U.S. District Court in Albuquerque how he said his father held out his badge on two occasions during the incident before Tafoya was arrested, after Tafoya and the sheriff struggled over the sheriff's gun. The sheriff also faces a firearms charge.

Charges against Rodella Jr. in the same incident were previously dismissed by the U.S. Attorney for medical reasons, stemming from a head injury the younger Rodella suffered while serving with the New Mexico National Guard in Kosovo. . .

A jogger who testified earlier in the case confirmed that Tafoya, from his car, asked the jogger to call police during the incident.

Rodella Jr. agreed under questioning from prosecutor Tara Neda that he was taking several psychotropic drugs and suffered from PTSD. He said he had few memory problems or problems with confusion, but said he did have some problems with irritability and concentration.

Neda asked him if he told his doctor that he was "so hyper vigilant" that he slept with a pistol. "Yes, I do sleep with it," he answered.

It is helpful to note at this point that Tommy Rodella Sr. has had a colorful career in both law enforcement and the judiciary. A career full of behavior that would have found most others in jail, as reported by Staff (2014):

Rodella was elected sheriff in 2010, despite having been ousted as a magistrate judge by the state Supreme Court two years earlier for misconduct. The court barred him from running again for judicial office.

He had been appointed as a magistrate in 2005 by then Gov. Bill Richardson, but resigned a few months later amid criticism—and pressure from Richardson—for helping secure the release of a family friend who had been jailed for drunken driving.

As a state police officer, Rodella was disciplined for marijuana use, improper use of a weapon, falsifying official reports, abusing sick leave and using his position for personal gain. He also was suspended for 30 days for firing at a deer decoy that game officers had set up to catch poachers.

Rodella served in the state police from 1982 until retiring in 1995 on a disability pension.

Rodella Sr. was ultimately convicted of two federal charges related to the Tafoya case: "a civil rights charge for making an unconstitutional arrest of a motorist and a firearms charge for brandishing a gun during the crime" (Stiny, 2014b).

Tommy Rodella Sr. is pictured (center) leaving the courthouse subsequent to his conviction.

This case, and the storied history of the Rodellas, raises a number of issues:

First, it highlights how steroids are connected with all manner of mental health issues, to say nothing of increased aggression. This by virtue of the facts in the Tafoya incident, and by virtue of Tommy Jr.'s own admissions about his mental state.

Second, it demonstrates fitness of duty issues that are often ignored in law enforcement culture. These in relation to prior incidents of criminal misconduct and the use of mind-altering prescription medication by those authorized to carry firearms and make life-and-death decisions. These considerations are too often ignored in law enforcement culture for a variety of financial and political reasons. This allows bad actors to infect law enforcement, all the way up the chain of command.

Finally, the matter of steroid abuse was not addressed in this case. Basic investigative questions beg answering when steroid use is uncovered, such as: Where did Tommy Jr. get his steroids? What was he using them for? Was this lawful use? What other drugs were found in his system? Was Tommy Sr. tested for drug use? What were the results? Was all of the drug use happening under Tommy Sr.'s watch and with his direct knowledge, given that Tommy Jr. was living at the family residence? How was Tommy Jr. able to remain in the National Guard, and pass an annual physical, given his condition and medication?

The answers to these questions, which may be posed in depositions as part of the eventual civil action in this case by Mr. Tafoya, would tend to increase departmental liability significantly depending on how they are answered. And depending on who knew what when. Additionally, the failure of law enforcement to investigate these issues fully, and hold those involved to account, gives the further impression of negligence and corruption.

CHAPTER 5

Profiles of Abuse and Addiction: Understanding the Adverse Side Effects of Anabolic Steroid Abuse

It is established that prolonged use of anabolic steroids in high doses leads to a host of severe physical and psychological side effects. In extreme cases, this can include sudden cardiac arrest and death (Trenton and Currier, 2005; Buttner and Thieme, 2010). None of the side effects of anabolic steroid abuse are conducive to wellness[1] or longevity; and many of them will mark the anabolic steroid abuser in an almost undeniable fashion.

This is something that the anabolic steroid addict will refute to the point of agitation and physical confrontation, which all but makes the point about the hazards of addiction. They will even go so far as to claim that available scientific data about the effects of anabolic steroid use is in conflict with itself, and that no conclusive evidence exists either way on the subject. However, when pressed they will not be able to give any scientific literature to support this position; rather, they will only be able to make vague references to pro-steroid websites, blogs, and related sales literature. That is because the scientific literature, as cited throughout this work, is very clear on the subject. Anyone claiming otherwise, whether or not they have a medical license, has simply not done their homework.

But these hollow denials are all beside the point. The profile of an anabolic steroid abuser is fairly straightforward. Most of those using them illegally are not engaged in low-dose or short-term therapy. They are often found abusing their drugs of choice at levels 10 times beyond that which is recommended, if not much more. They are also generally found to be abusing for a period of years before suspicions of abuse

---

[1] *Wellness* is often described as good physical and mental health.

can be investigated and proved. This typically occurs when they can no longer hide the volume of drugs being taken, the amount of money they are spending, or the severity of their physical and psychological symptoms. To be clear, this is because all chronic steroid abuse leads to severe adverse side effects of some kind, and every community of abuser-addicts knows this.

When considering the adverse side effects of anabolic steroid abuse, it is also helpful to understand that anabolic steroids may be administered in a variety of ways. They may be taken orally, in the form of a pill; they may be injected as a liquid directly into the bloodstream with a needle; or they may be applied topically by rubbing a steroid cream on the skin.

The method of delivery may have its own side effects. For example, most anabolic steroid abusers use a needle and syringe. They inject themselves with a liquid to get the quickest and most concentrated dosage with the least amount of loss. Carelessness and incapability can result in injury and infection. If needle sharing occurs, this increases the risk of infection and transmitting blood born diseases such as hepatitis and HIV.

The side effects profiled in this section are taken from the literature, including, but not limited to, AGSSG (2011); Buttner and Thieme (2010); CSAT (2006); Daley and Ellis (1994); DEA (2004); Grogan et al. (2006); Humphrey et al. (2008); Sweitzer (2004); Trenton and Currier (2005).

5.1 SIDE EFFECTS: MALE SPECIFIC

In males, adverse side effects include:

- Breast enlargement
- Shrunken testicles
- Decreased sperm count to the point of sterility
- Impotence (i.e., the inability to achieve or maintain an erection)
- An enlarged prostate
- Lower back pain
- Water retention.

5.2 SIDE EFFECTS: FEMALE SPECIFIC

In females, adverse side effects include:

- Breast shrinkage[2]
- Facial hair growth[3]
- Extreme clitoral enlargement[4]
- Menstrual irregularity (e.g., spotty or nonexistent periods).

5.3 SIDE EFFECTS: UNIVERSAL

The following are common adverse side effects of anabolic steroid abuse suffered by both males and females, categorized into physical, injection-related, and psychological.

5.3.1 Physical

Adverse physical side effects commonly suffered by both males and females include:

- Decreased libido (sex drive)
- Deepened voice[5]
- Headaches
- Kidney pain
- General skin infections and skin tearing
- Straie (stretch marks)
- Alopecia (baldness)
- Severe acne on the face and back
- Uticaria (hives)
- Liver disease
- Kidney damage
- Gastrointestinal distress
- Severe eczema[6]
- Increased heart size

[2]Many female anabolic steroid abusers eventually get breast implants because the loss of breast fat is so complete.

[3]Many female steroid abusers gain so much facial hair that they eventually turn to laser treatments in order to permanently deal with the problem.

[4]The clitoris often grows out as much as an inch, even more, resembling a very small penis.

[5]This is caused by tissue thickening around the neck and vocal cords, and is perhaps more immediately noticeable in female anabolic steroid abusers.

[6]Some anabolic steroids are applied to the skin as a cream, and prolonged use can result in painful patches of dry, cracked skin on the hands and in the area of application.

- Increased risk of high blood pressure, heart disease, and stroke
- Sudden cardiac death.

5.3.2 Injection Related
Adverse physical side effects related to drug injection commonly suffered by both males and females include:

- Neurovascular injury (damage to blood vessels and nerve clusters)
- Hematoma (a.k.a. ecchymosis or bruising)
- Fibrosis (a.k.a. scarring)
- Bacterial infection
- Hepatitis B or C
- HIV infection.

5.3.3 Psychological
Adverse psychological side effects commonly suffered by both males and females include:

- Psychological dependance and addiction
- Rapid mood swings
- Short-term personality changes during periods of increased use
- Increased aggression (a.k.a. "roid rage")[7]
- Paranoia[8]
- Mania[9]
- Delusions of grandeur
- Psychosis[10]
- Irrational thoughts and behavior
- Memory loss
- Panic attacks

[7]Aggression can manifest as uncontrolled anger, combativeness, or hostility. That is to say, it can be both physical and verbal. Either suggests psychological distress.

[8]Increased paranoia may be a product of increased aggression combined with participation in an ongoing criminal enterprise that must be constantly covered up with lies, and the related fear of discovery, termination, arrest, and jail time.

[9]*Mania* is described in Humphrey et al. (2008) as: "high energy levels associated with increased self-confidence, increased activity, impaired judgment, and reckless behavior." Mania can be evident by increased activity, fast talking at an elevated volume, racing thoughts, and decreased social appropriateness. Those engaged in manic behavior are the least able to recognize it; those who are around it all the time may come to accept it as the norm and are the least likely to report it. These kinds of psychological symptoms are often best observed and reported by someone that does not work with the subject on a daily basis, if at all.

[10]*Psychosis* is a lack of contact with, or awareness of, reality. It can include all manner of sensory hallucinations or distorted perceptions.

- Severe depression
- Suicidal thoughts and tendencies.

5.4 RED FLAGS INDICATIVE OF ANABOLIC STEROID ABUSE

Based on the research conducted by the authors in preparation for this work, including the references cited and the case examples provided throughout, the following red flags have emerged as indicators of anabolic steroid abuse by public safety employees:

- High muscle mass and definition, in combination with low body fat
- Disproportionate muscle development to body size
- Disproportionate muscle development in the upper body
- Severe acne or eczema, especially on the face, neck or back
- Rapid muscle gain
- Compulsive weightlifting without getting tired
- Use of multiple nutritional supplements
- Participation in competitive body building
- Rapid mood swings and erratic behavior
- Lack of professional boundaries
- An absence of good or rational judgment
- History of excessive force complaints or concealing use of force incidents
- History of reprimands and suspensions
- A known history of anabolic steroid use, abuse, procurement, or dealing[11]
- Association with illegal drug dealers in their personal life.

As these are red flags, the existence of one or more of these indicators suggests the need for further investigation and testing. Failure to require public safety employees to submit to random drug testing when these indicators are present can lead to a failure to prevent misconduct, injury, wrongful death, and potential agency liability.

5.5 CONCLUSION

Prolonged use of anabolic steroids, especially in high doses can result in a host of harmful physical and psychological side effects, including death. These vary depending on the abuser's sex, method of application,

---

[11]An agency that retains employees with this type of background is asking to be sued.

dosage, duration of use, and synergy with other drugs. Those who abuse anabolic steroids will focus on short-term performance and image-enhancement benefits while denying, and concealing, any adverse side effects. However, these denials ring hollow as severe adverse side effects are often apparent to even the most casual observer.

There are numerous red flags for anabolic steroid abuse that should be readily apparent to public safety supervisors and leaders. Failure to monitor for these indicators, and require testing when they are present, is evidence of agency negligence. Consequently, those agencies seeking to maintain the public trust and avoid liability will attend to these considerations as a routine matter.

Case Example
Lt. Scott Ghidoni, Barnstable County Sheriff's Office

During the month of May 2014, Lt. Scott Ghidoni of the Barnstable County Sheriff's Office in Massachusetts was arrested twice. First he was arrested for assaulting his domestic partner. As reported in Cassidy (2014):

Police were called to a reported domestic disturbance on Watercure Street at about 10 p.m. April 24, according to a police report filed in Plymouth District Court.

The caller said she had a verbal altercation with Scott Ghidoni, 42, and she feared the situation was going to escalate, according to the report...

Officers then spoke with the woman, who said Ghidoni had yelled at her for watching television in their shared bedroom, according to the report. She said that when she continued to watch the program on her mobile phone he left the room but came back, according to the report. "Scott Ghidoni got into bed with her, grabbed her by her arms, and started shaking her, yelling, and requesting that he wanted her to hit/ strike him," the officer wrote.

There were no marks on the woman's arms and she declined treatment, according to the report.

Police arrested Ghidoni and charged him with domestic assault and battery. Police also seized a Glock 19 9 mm handgun, nine magazines, 50 rounds of 9 mm ammunition and a canister of pepper spray, according to the report.

An abuse prevention order was issued against Ghidoni, according to police.

Lt. Ghidoni denied any physical altercation, but admitted there had been a heated verbal argument.

Barnstable County Sheriff's Lt. Scott Ghidoni photographed outside of a Dollar Tree store in May 2014, from Facebook.

Subsequent to Lt. Ghidoni's arrest and the related protective order, an officer from the Barnstable County Sheriff's Office called the victim to arrange for his personal items to be picked up from her residence. She informed the officer that there was a safe in her home that contained steroids and syringes belonging to Lt. Ghidoni. As further reported in Cassidy (2014):

> *Officers went to the apartment and they took the safe to the police station, according to the report. Ghidoni was called into the station and asked if the safe was his and whether officers could search it, which he said they could, according to the report.*
> *"The safe was opened in Scott's presence," according to the report. "Inside were numerous vials of testosterone and syringes. When asked about the items Scott stated that two of the vials were his but that they were old. He denied owning any other items in the safe."*

Lt. Ghidoni, a nearly 16-year veteran of the department, was arrested a second time for illegal possession of steroids. He was also subsequently suspended without pay, pending the outcome of his criminal court proceedings.

It is hard to imagine an outcome in this case that does not involve termination, as Lt. Ghidoni has admitted to a crime (illegal steroid possession), and the other charges against him involve domestic violence. Conviction on either offense would cause him to lose the right to carry a firearm.

It is important to note that, in this case, the Barnstable County Sheriff's Office acted appropriately across the board. The next steps should involve administering a drug test, to include steroids, on Lt. Ghidoni to determine current levels and usage; determining where Lt. Ghidoni acquired his illegal steroids (e.g., police evidence storage, Internet, roid mill, coworker, or illegal drug dealer); determining whether any other officers in the department are using illegal steroids; and drug testing everyone in the department to remove the stain of Lt. Ghidoni's misconduct.[12]

Case Example
Chris Benoit, Pro Wrestler and Dr. Phil Astin, III

On June 25, 2007, the bodies of professional wrestler Chris Benoit (40), his wife Nancy (43),[13] and their son, Daniel (7) were discovered at their home in Fayetteville, GA. Local police found them while conducting a welfare check initiated by concerned friends and colleagues. Benoit had previously claimed his wife was seriously ill, and he had also missed his flights to attend major professional wrestling events. Then he just stopped responding to those people trying to help him keep his schedule.

Professional wrestler Chris Benoit, a.k.a. The Crippler.

The police investigation would ultimately reveal that Chris Benoit killed both his wife and son, and then he killed himself. Investigators

---

[12]This could require a proffer agreement with prosecutors, in which the person under investigation gives information about the others involved without fear of prosecution. It is not necessarily a granting of complete immunity, and it can also be used against the witness if they lie about or omit details regarding their other involvement in criminal activity.

[13]Of note is the fact that Nancy Benoit also performed as a pro wrestler, but that part of her career ended in the late 1990s.

also found prescription anabolic steroids and other medication in his home. Scott Ballard, the Fayette County District Attorney, gave a detailed account of the crimes in a statement to the press:

— Before going home on Friday, Chris Benoit went to see his doctor, Phil Astin of Atlanta, regarding his testosterone prescription.
— On Friday evening, Nancy Benoit was asphyxiated with a cord around her neck, and her body "was found in an upstairs family room with her legs and wrists bound and blood under her head, perhaps indicating a struggle" (Fox, 2007).
— On Saturday morning, Daniel Benoit was asphyxiated in his bedroom. He was reported to have been killed by a specific type of wrestling chokehold, and was also reported to have been unconscious during the attack (ABC, 2007).
— On Sunday morning, Chris Benoit went into his home gym and hung himself using a cable attached to a weight machine.

Both Nancy and Daniel were found with bibles placed beside their bodies.

Nancy Benoit as her pro wrestling alter-ego "Fallen Angel," in the years before her marriage to Chris Benoit.

Ultimately, toxicology reports revealed that Chris Benoit's body had 10 times the normal level of testosterone in it, along with Xanax (anti-anxiety) and Hydrocodone (painkiller). The medical examiner, Dr. Kris

Sperry of the Georgia Bureau of Investigation (GBI), opined that the testosterone had been injected shortly before Benoit's death.

Toxicology reports also revealed that Nancy Benoit had therapeutic (a.k.a. normal) levels of sedatives in her system, and that Daniel was sedated when he was killed.

In 2007, Dr. Phillip Astin, III, was arrested by federal investigators for his involvement in selling illegal prescriptions.

In 2009, he made a plea deal: 10 years in federal prison for 175 counts of illegally dispensing prescription drugs from 2002 until his 2007 arrest. As reported in Crosby (2009):

> *According to United States Attorney Nahmias and the information in court: On January 29, 2009, ASTIN pleaded guilty to offenses relating to 19 patients who received hundreds of illegal prescriptions for methadone, Percocet, Oxycontin, M.S. Contin, Demerol, Lorcet, Ritalin, Vicodin, Klonopin, Vicoprofen, Xanax, Adderall, and Soma.*
>
> *Through his plea agreement, ASTIN further admitted that the prescriptions he issued resulted in the death of one patient when she overdosed on the drugs. Finally, ASTIN admitted that he wrote and filled 16 prescriptions for Lortab, Xanax, Dexedrine, Adderall, and Ritalin in the names of two patients without their knowledge.*
>
> *During the sentencing hearing today, prosecutors and witnesses described the scope of ASTIN's illegal conduct, which involved dozens of patients and illegal prescriptions for abused drugs from as early as 1999. Some patients received popularly abused painkillers, amphetamines, anxiety medications, and muscle relaxers for more than five years without a legitimate medical examination, diagnosis, or monitoring by ASTIN. A pharmacologist explained the severe damage that these drugs inflict upon the body, as well as the overwhelming physical and psychological dependence that results from abusing the drugs.*
>
> *According to the evidence presented during the sentencing hearing, from approximately May 2002 until the date of his arrest in July 2007, ASTIN intentionally wrote prescriptions for controlled substances that were not for a legitimate medical purpose and were not in the usual course of a doctor's professional practice. ASTIN dispensed these prescriptions without conducting the appropriate physical examinations and diagnoses to justify the prescriptions and, as a result, many of the patients who received these illegitimate prescriptions became addicts. The evidence showed that ASTIN's notoriety grew among pill-abusing patients from across Georgia, Alabama, and other states, as well as professional wrestlers.*
>
> *ASTIN also admitted to writing multiple prescriptions for the same drug on the same date, sometimes as many as four simultaneous Percocet prescriptions to the same patient for the same 30-day period, and wrote undated prescriptions as well. Federal law requires medical*

practitioners to sign and date each prescription for controlled substances on the date that it is issued. Finally, ASTIN dispensed methadone as a maintenance therapy without the proper license to dispense drugs in this fashion and in quantities and durations that readily perpetuated the addiction of these patients.

The evidence presented at the sentencing hearing included descriptions of several of the patients to whom ASTIN wrote illegal drugs. On June 20, 2007, one patient overdosed on Lortab, Xanax, and Soma that were prescribed by ASTIN and died from acute toxicity of the drugs, and prosecutors further described another patient who died, in part, from an overdose of Soma that had been prescribed by ASTIN. Other evidence included instances where ASTIN was alerted to the abuse and addiction of certain patients, yet continued to give them prescriptions for years.

The evidence showed that a professional wrestler said that it was widely known in the professional wrestling community that ASTIN would dispense prescriptions without performing a medical examination. This patient received prescription drugs, including Lorcet, Percocet, Xanax, and Soma, from ASTIN from December 2004 until November 2005, and said that he did not receive a legitimate medical examination or testing from ASTIN during that time. The wrestler developed an addiction to the drugs, and ASTIN never questioned his addiction and instead simply wrote prescriptions for larger quantities of pills. The patient said that his girlfriend at the time and a number of professional wrestlers obtained prescription drugs from ASTIN for the purpose of abusing the drugs, adding that some of these wrestlers also were addicted to the drugs.

Prosecutors emphasized that these patients comprised only a portion of patients to whom ASTIN gave illegal prescriptions.

Dr. Astin is also linked to the Cobb County police and firefighter steroid abuse scandal out of Georgia. Dr. Astin is known to have provided questionable prescriptions to one of the firefighters at the center of this scandal, Philip Wilbur, prior to his federal arrest.[14] However, Dr. Astin is by no means alone in that regard.

[14]The Cobb County Georgia steroid abuse scandal is discussed in Chapter 7.

CHAPTER 6

Motivations and Rationalizations: The Psychology of Anabolic Steroid Abuse

We have explained that anabolic steroid abuse is generally motivated by the desire to get physically bigger, to reduce body fat, and to increase muscle definition. It is a matter of looks and performance. At least, that's how it starts. However, these superficial physical results do not adequately explain the underlying psychological issues that are more often at play. The reality is that when you are looking at someone abusing anabolic steroids, you are looking at someone with extremely low self-esteem, a substance abuse problem, and perhaps even a mental disorder.

This chapter will explore these and related issues.[1]

6.1 LOW SELF-ESTEEM

Low self-esteem refers to an overall lack of confidence in oneself and one's abilities. It is evidenced by persistent self-doubt, envy, negativity, self-deprecation, self-sabotage, and the inability to recognize personal achievement or accomplishment. Those with chronic low self-esteem are resistant to compliments and always see the worst in things. They are also unable to identify and appreciate their own success. In addition, they are easily devastated by, and can react unpredictably to, the slightest criticism from others—even complete strangers.

Low self-esteem is accompanied by frustration, hostility, and aggression. It is also found in association with a host of mental health diagnoses and disorders, including mania, depression, chronic anxiety, narcissism, eating disorders, and body disorders. It can result in a continuum of

---

[1]Anabolic steroid abuse is often discussed in relation to body *dysmorphic disorder*, which is a psychiatric condition characterized by those who worry about their body image (e.g., shape, size, and dimensions) to the point of delusion. Such cases are incredibly rare. However, they are also covered by the discussions in this chapter as they share the same underlying psychological issue: chronic low self-esteem.

individual coping mechanisms, running the spectrum between social withdrawal and extreme exhibitionism or competitiveness.[2]

Paradoxically, those with low self-esteem may outwardly project a veneer of exaggerated joy and confidence. This is a common coping mechanism referred to as overcompensation. It is also associated with bipolar disorder and manic-depression.

Along this line, there are those who join law enforcement to compensate for personal feelings of loss, powerlessness, and inadequacy. These individuals are particularly vulnerable to substance abuse and addiction. They become even more prone to steroid abuse as they seek to fit in with other officers in new assignments that are juicing; or as they get older, losing their youthful vitality and appearance.

6.2 PERFORMANCE ENHANCEMENT

Performance enhancement means just that. The belief is that anabolic steroids are an easy way to get stronger and faster. This can help public safety officers during annual performance evaluations and physicals, in terms of maintaining their weight, strength, and endurance.

Additionally, anabolic steroids are believed to provide a competitive edge over the aggressive suspects and criminals that officers encounter. Perhaps this is why anabolic steroid abuse is common among those in high-aggression assignments, such as Gang and SWAT units. Those serving in these units tend to emphasize masculinity, prioritizing physical intimidation and aggression as a legitimate means to an end, even among female members. As reported in DEA (2004, p. 5):

> ...individuals in occupations requiring enhanced physical strength (body guards, construction workers, and law enforcement officers) are known to take these drugs. Steroids are purported to increase lean body mass, strength and aggressiveness. Steroids are also believed to reduce recovery time between workouts, which makes it possible to train harder and thereby further improve strength and endurance. As a result of these claims, others, including law enforcement personnel, have used steroids for personal and professional reasons.

[2]Shyness and exhibitionism are opposite sides of the same coin, originating from feelings of extremely low self-esteem. They manifest as the fear of rejection to the point of social avoidance at one end of the spectrum, all the way to the need for approval to the point of doing anything (even the most degrading acts) for acceptance.

The law enforcement profession is both mentally and physically challenging. As a result, law enforcement personnel seek remedies and solutions to perform their daily tasks more effectively. Anabolic steroids are a drug of choice because they are known for increasing the size and strength of muscles more quickly and easily, and increasing one's endurance while performing physical activities. Some law enforcement personnel may believe that steroids provide them a physical and psychological advantage while performing their jobs.

This message is echoed in the warnings offered by Humphrey et al. (2008):

Unlike with other forms of drug abuse, steroid users do not take their drug recreationally; on the contrary, some state they need these drugs in order to do their job effectively or improve their "job performance." From street officers who consider themselves vulnerable to bigger, more aggressive criminals to special assignment officers who are regularly tested for their physical abilities, officers are turning to performance-enhancing drugs such as AASs and HGH as a shortcut to improved performance.

Despite the common belief that using anabolic steroids can make an officer the best they can be, the reality is much different. As already explained, while short-term physical gains are likely, there are long-term physical and psychological consequences that result from abuse. From a rational perspective, these adverse effects far outweigh any short-term benefits. However, an addict can convince themselves of anything, and they rarely confine themselves to a safe regimen. They just want to keep getting bigger, no matter the professional, financial, or personal cost.

6.3 VANITY: IMAGE ENHANCEMENT

Losing weight or increasing muscle mass and definition via anabolic steroid abuse is partially about looking good, or at least perceiving that one looks good to those one is trying to impress.

Ultimately, being ego driven, those who want to look good will then want the results of their efforts to be seen. This means they may like wearing revealing or form-fitting clothing. It also means that they may desperately want to have their picture taken, either by themselves or others.

This tends to involve seeking out venues for self-display. For some this can be satisfied by posting a succession of revealing "selfies" on social networking sites, or by excessive partying or night clubbing. For others, it can involve extreme sports and competitive weightlifting where they seek trophies, audience approval, and the possibility of temporary celebrity through media coverage. Either way, what they want is to be the center of attention, with all eyes on them in awe.

In small doses, this can be a form of healthy self-expression. Being recognized for achievement is a good thing; getting the approval of people that one respects for healthy accomplishments is one of the ways we become motivated to improve ourselves. But needing that approval or attention in order to be whole, and engaging in risky or self-destructive behavior to get it is something else entirely.

In extreme cases, chronic vanity is a reflection of pathological narcissism. As explained by the Mayo Clinic (2014b):

> Narcissistic personality disorder is a mental disorder in which people have an inflated sense of their own importance and a deep need for admiration. Those with narcissistic personality disorder believe that they're superior to others and have little regard for other people's feelings. But behind this mask of ultra-confidence lies a fragile self-esteem, vulnerable to the slightest criticism.

The delusion of physical perfection afforded by anabolic steroid abuse (that it is both healthy and attainable) is overwhelming, to the point where even the most rational mind can become lost to it. This makes talking to the vanity-motivated abuser an exercise in futility. They are often so enamored with the end result that they can learn to rationalize, and deny, anything. Ultimately, anabolic steroid abuse turns the egotist into a vain liar that is chasing an unobtainable fantasy at the cost of everything else in their life.[3]

6.4 FEAR FACTOR

Another common motivation for the anabolic steroid abuser is the fear factor. The bigger they get, the more physically imposing they become. This speaks to their need to project a hulking image that is intended to frighten and intimidate others.

---

[3]The financial cost of anabolic steroid abuse is not small, and can cause abusers to engage in illegal activity to maintain their usage. This has been demonstrated by several of the examples in this work. The financial toll that anabolic steroid abuse takes on an individual and their family is not so very different than any other form of drug abuse. Obviously, this cannot be discounted as a contributing stressor with respect to the more extreme consequences of anabolic steroid abuse.

The motivation to get big can come from initial size inadequacies, with respect to a public safety officer that feels too short, too small, or too skinny. However, this need can also come from the anxiety of prior loss, defeat, or trauma. As reported in NIDA (2006, p. 3):

> Some people who abuse steroids to boost muscle size have experienced physical or sexual abuse. In one series of interviews with male weightlifters, 25 percent who abused steroids reported memories of childhood physical or sexual abuse. Similarly, female weightlifters who had been raped were found to be twice as likely to report use of anabolic steroids or another purported muscle building drug, compared with those who had not been raped. Moreover, almost all of those who had been raped reported that they markedly increased their bodybuilding activities after the attack. They believed that being bigger and stronger would discourage further attacks because men would find them either intimidating or unattractive.

This rationale, and the cycle of anabolic steroid abuse, is further discussed in James (2007):

> In the police community, cultural acceptance of bodybuilding and access to online suppliers make it easier for officers to obtain steroids...
>
> "Some of it is real and some of it is imagined on the part of the officers involved: fear, anxiety, wanting to do a better job," said [Gene Sanders, police psychologist from Spokane, WA], who consults with physicians across the country as director of the Police Stress Institute. The temptation to find a "quick fix" is always present, said Sanders. Several older studies have placed police officers at the "bottom of the fitness scale," below firefighters and out-ranked by inmates, he said.
>
> "The body feels really comfortable and likes [the hormones]," said Sanders. "You feel better, feel more buff and feel more able to take on the bad people."
>
> Indeed, Matthew[4] felt the positive effects of steroids after only three months' use. His weight jumped from 170 pounds to 192 pounds, and he was able to bench-press 300 pounds from 225 pounds...
>
> "I was incredibly stronger," he said. "I never felt healthier in my life and woke up full of energy and felt it throughout the day. Never once did I feel out of control."
>
> "Maybe I was a little edgier," he added. "The kids got me upset a little more and I was less tolerant, but never to the point where I would physically do anyone harm."

---

[4]James (2007) reports that "Matthew" is a "six-year veteran of a Pennsylvania police force patrolling an area encroached upon by urban crime" that prefers to remain anonymous. Matthew reportedly turned to steroids after a bad encounter trying to subdue a "crazed youth." Eventually, Matthew's illegal drug use was found out, he was forced to resign, and he spent 23 days in jail.

> ...*Still, said Sanders, steroid users tend to think "more is better" and don't know where to draw the line as they build bulk. Users typically combine steroids with a combination of drugs in a phenomenon known as "stacking," and "cycle" on and off the drugs to avoid building a tolerance.*
>
> *"They can go from being calm and collected to raging bulls," said Sanders. "There is also a subcategory of these folks like the crazy Vietnam veteran. They think that if they appear crazy, people will back off."*

The reality is that more anabolic steroids are not better, they are simply more dangerous in terms of both fostering addiction and increasing the severity (and permanency) of other adverse side effects.

6.5 RATIONALIZATIONS

In order to engage in illegal anabolic steroid abuse, the public safety officer has to rationalize illegal drug use and procurement against their public safety role. The following is a list of the most common rationalizations encountered by the authors. All of them ring hollow, and none of them provide a legitimate administrative or criminal defense:

1. I need anabolic steroids to keep my edge.
2. I need them to keep my job.
3. I need them to keep safe.
4. Everyone else is juicing so I have to, in order to stay competitive or just fit in.
5. Everyone else is juicing so it's OK, even if I get caught.
6. Steroids are made by my body, so they can't really be harmful.
7. I don't think using anabolic steroids should be illegal.
8. Anabolic steroids aren't as bad as other drugs, so juicing is no big deal.
9. Anabolic steroids are legal if I can get a doctor's prescription.
10. I only juice when I need to.
11. I can handle my dosage; I know how to manage it.
12. I'm only hurting myself.
13. If I stop using anabolic steroids now, I will shrink back down to nothing.

It is important to understand that the anabolic steroid abuser in public safety cannot successfully rationalize an addiction without the support of those in his personal life and his agency. Public safety leadership must also be willing to rationalize what they see every day in terms of illegal activity and adverse behavior by the addict. Common supervisor and leadership rationalizations include:

1. Steroids make my officers look good and perform better.
2. It's only steroids; it's no big deal.
3. I don't have an obligation to go looking for trouble in my department.
4. Everyone else is doing steroids so I can't single one employee out.
5. Everyone else is doing steroids so if I turn them all in I won't have a department.
6. I've invested too much time and money in the employee; it's just cheaper to look the other way.

Again, all of these rationalizations ring hollow, and none of them provides a legitimate administrative or criminal defense to supervisory negligence and ignoring criminal activity.

6.6 CONCLUSION

Anabolic steroid abusers suffer from low self-esteem, sometimes to the point of delusion and even mental illness. However, this can manifest itself in a variety of ways, and may even result in overcompensation in one form or another. Anabolic steroid abusers in law enforcement are prone to a number of related motivations and rationalizations, including performance enhancement, image enhancement, and the desire to frighten and intimidate others. Additionally, public safety leadership often participates in these rationalizations and fails to act, for their own reasons.

None of these rationalizations make anabolic steroid abuse less of an addiction or a crime. None of them can protect the public safety officer from the adverse side effects of long-term abuse. And none of them can protect the agency from the liabilities that can result from anabolic steroid abuse.

Case Example
Officer Abbegayle Dorn, Denver Police Department, CO

Officer Abbegayle Dorn of the Denver Police Department in Colorado was also a bodybuilder and professional fitness model. She appeared on the TV show *American Gladiators* in 2008, and her images can still be found on a number of bodybuilding websites. However, things began to fall apart when she became the target of a lawsuit alleging excessive force, as reported by Bunch (2010):

Officer Abbegayle Dorn of the Denver Police Department was known for fitness modeling and bodybuilding.

A federal lawsuit filed this week alleges a female Denver police officer responding to a loud music complaint "tortured" a 23-year-old man and trashed a group of partygoers' cellphones after they recorded her actions. The officer, Abbegayle Dorn, has had a high profile as a professional fitness model and a 2008 contestant on the TV show "American Gladiator."

The suit, reported by KCNC News4, targets Dorn, two male officers the plaintiff did not know and the Denver Police Department. It's the latest in a series of brutality claims against the department. The city attorney's office reported this month that the city had paid out nearly $6.2 million since 2004 to settle lawsuits involving police officers. Almost all of them involved allegations of excessive force.

In the suit filed Tuesday, Rohit Mukherjee also said an unidentified officer at the Denver County Jail referred to him as a "(expletive) Arab." Mukherjee is of Indian descent.

The suit alleges police violated Mukherjee's Fourth Amendment rights with an unlawful arrest. The suit also alleges he was "tortured" by police despite giving no resistance other than to cry out in pain. Mukherjee was celebrating with nine friends in his 17th Street apartment April 10 before he was to leave for a business apprenticeship in India.

His attorney, Alan Molk, would not comment on the suit, except to say Dorn's gender was not a factor. "It doesn't make any difference whatsoever that she's a woman," he said. "A police officer has the same duties and responsibilities, regardless of gender."

...The suit claims that when Dorn and the two male officers came to Mukherjee's door shortly before midnight April 10, he hesitated before stepping into the hallway, prompting a male officer to force open the door, and Dorn pinned Mukherjee's neck against it. Mukherjee claims he was forced to the ground face first, then dragged from a vinyl floor to carpet in a "wheelbarrow-like fashion," causing scrapes to his face. Dorn then stood on his ankle, Mukherjee alleges.

When Dorn saw some of the partygoers taking photos and video, she took their phones, went to the kitchen and put them in a bowl of water, the lawsuit states. The suit also claims officers twisted Mukherjee's fingers as they questioned him, kneed him in the head and smashed his face into the wall as they walked him out, while taunting him.

Seven of the nine people at the party, five men and two women, were originally charged with either disturbing the peace or interfering with a police officer, but all those charges were dismissed by the Denver district attorney, the suit states. Mukherjee was charged with assault on a police officer, resisting arrest, disturbing the peace and interfering with a police officer. Those charges also were dropped.

According to the plaintiff's attorney, this particular lawsuit was settled by the Denver Police Department in 2011 for $30,000.00.

Officer Dorn posed for a number of professional photo shoots, including, ironically, this one for the clothing line "Illegal Street Wear".

Officer Dorn was subsequently investigated by the FBI for illegal anabolic steroid use and procurement. While no criminal charges were filed, the Denver Police Department continued with their own internal investigation into her behavior. She was removed from the streets and placed on administrative duty in 2013. Ultimately, in June 2013, Dorn resigned from the department and the police investigation into her anabolic steroid abuse ended (Gurman, 2013). It appears likely that she was given the same choice that many in law enforcement are afforded when confronted with evidence of criminal misconduct, including illegal anabolic steroid abuse: resign or face termination.

Case Example
Officer Richard Klementovich, Clifton Police Department, NJ

In June 2012, on Father's Day, Officer Richard Klementovich of the Clifton Police Department in New Jersey was engaged in a 10-h standoff against police at his estranged wife's home. He called the police himself and left a note on the front door for them which stated, among other things: "I served in the last Persian Gulf war. I have about 2000 rounds. I have come here to die." As reported in Hegel and Coughlin (2012):

Officer Richard Klementovich enjoyed posting on-duty pictures of himself on social media, such as this one.

One police officer was injured and two police cars were damaged during a 10-hour Father's Day standoff that ended peacefully shortly before midnight with the surrender of an off-duty New Jersey police officer on Bittersweet Drive in Doylestown Township.

The suspect, 42-year-old Richard Klementovich, a decorated officer with the Clifton police force, was taken into custody on the front lawn of his wife's home at 11:45 p.m. Sunday while wearing a bulletproof vest and a gas mask.

Police said Klementovich had contacted his wife, who had filed for divorce last year, earlier Sunday to meet her and their children else-where for Father's Day. Instead of meeting them, he entered his wife's empty home and barricaded himself inside.

The drama began at 1:44 p.m. Sunday when police got a call about a neighborhood dispute involving Klementovich, according to Dave Mettin, Pennridge Regional police chief and an administrator with Central Bucks SWAT.

At 1:58 p.m., shots were fired at police who responded to the scene, he said. One officer was injured by shrapnel, and two police vehicles were hit by gunfire, Mettin said. Another round of gunfire was heard about 4 p.m. and again about 5 p.m., police said. Another officer said the injured police officer was hit in the face by shrapnel after a gunshot hit a curb. Identified as Doylestown Borough police Cpl. William Doucette, he was taken to Doylestown Hospital and released. Police said an armored vehicle was also damaged by gunfire from Klementovich.

...Mettin said the suspect surrendered after speaking with a nego-tiator from the Central Bucks emergency response team. Police took him into custody in the front yard without further incident and took him back to the township police station for processing late Sunday night...

Neighbors said they believe Klementovich recently moved out of the home on Bittersweet, which he shared with two children and his wife. According to court records, the home was purchased by Klementovich and Jill Majors in 2006. In December 2011, the ownership changed to Majors alone.

Klementovich is a decorated officer and fitness buff in "top physical shape," according to retired Clifton police Lt. Pat Ciser who worked midnight shifts with him. Ciser, who said Klementovich just went through a bitter divorce, spoke with The Record newspaper based in Bergen County, NJ.

Klementovich was sworn in as an officer of the Clifton force in January 1998 and earns a salary of $102,752 there. He's a Desert Storm veteran and served with the Army Airborne, police said.

Officer Richard Klementovich surrendered to police at his estranged wife's home after a 10-h Father's Day standoff with police.

Officer Klementovich had been out of work for about 2 months with a back injury prior to the standoff. Initially, he was charged with 14 counts of attempted murder, in addition to multiple counts of aggravated assault and reckless endangerment. However, he was eventually able to make a deal with prosecutors, pleading no contest to one consolidated count of attempted murder. As reported in Petrick (2013), the adverse effects of steroid abuse were a feature of his defense:

> *The decorated Persian Gulf veteran was immediately sentenced by a judge to a sentence of 8½ to 20 years in prison, as negotiated under the plea agreement.*
>
> *Klementovich faced six counts of attempted homicide for allegedly firing at police officers, injuring one of them, and damaging several vehicles. Those six counts were "consolidated" into one count of attempted murder that named all the officers targeted, for the purposes of the plea, said defense attorney Jeff Simms of Passaic.*
>
> *None of those officers spoke during the sentencing, said Assistant District Attorney Nate Spang. But they have all been shocked by the experience. "It is something they train for. They know this type of scenario can occur," Spang said. "Thankfully, no one was seriously injured after it was over, but it was a sobering experience for a lot of them."*
>
> *The 14-year veteran of the Clifton Police Department barricaded himself in his wife's home in Doylestown on June 17, Father's Day, with a large stock of weapons and ammunition...*

"It was never his intention to harm a police officer. It was a serious cry for help," Simms said outside court Thursday. "He was so distraught between his steroid involvement, his post-traumatic stress and the breakup of his family that he didn't have any way to go, as far as he was concerned."

However, Klementovich indicated in a note to police and an email to his wife that he wanted to die in the standoff, according to officials. Klementovich, who was in the process of a divorce, also told his wife that he was angry about his job and had used steroids. . .

Simms said he had planned at trial to present a "diminished capacity" defense. "That means he was not clearly thinking," Simms said. "His emotions did not lead him in a clearly thinking pattern. He was only thinking of suicide and not of harming anybody but himself. And so, his ability to comprehend reality was diminished."

As part of the terms of his sentence, the judge explicitly ordered that former officer Klementovich was barred from using anabolic steroids while in prison, as reported in 2013.

In entering the plea, he abandoned an insanity defense he was expected to mount at trial. [Judge] Boylan ordered Klementovich to pay $69,016 in restitution, the cost of repairing and replacing vehicles damaged in the melee. She also ordered him to serve 17 years of probation and banned him from using steroids. Klementovich must comply with a mental health treatment plan in prison.

Klementovich, originally intent on committing suicide by cop, stated in a June 16, 2012, email to his ex-wife that he was angry "at this job and law enforcement. And it's them who I will take out my anger on. . . They will do the job I couldn't and take my life. . . I hope whomever comes to our house is ready to die tomorrow because I will be. . . Tell the police I have a surprise for them, this is the way I want to die." Now, according to police, he has agreed to be interviewed while in prison to help improve the way that hostage negotiators are trained.

CHAPTER 7

Scandals and Consequence: Exploring Anabolic Steroid Abuse in Public Safety

There have been dozens of steroid abuse scandals in public safety agencies throughout the United States since 2004 (e.g., the Jonesborough Police Department; the Lebanon Correctional Institute; the Manatee County Sheriff's Officer and the Manatee County Fire Rescue; the Memphis Police Department; and the Scottsboro Police Department[1]). In fact, once readers start looking, it will likely be difficult not to see these incidents everywhere. Hopefully, the increased identification and reporting of these cases is a result of investigators and supervisors becoming more aware of the illegalities and liabilities associated with anabolic steroid abuse.

In this chapter, we will briefly discuss the extent and consequences of some of those scandals that made it into the public domain. It is important to understand that not every law enforcement scandal is made public, and not every public scandal is covered by the press. More importantly, not all of them are fully investigated or even acknowledged by the agencies involved. Some just fade with media coverage as public safety agencies do their best to keep a lid on things through terminations, transfers, and modified duty.

Consequently, the cases discussed in this chapter serve as examples only, and are meant to show the varied responses that public safety agencies can have to organized crime, and drug dealing, within their ranks.

7.1 BOSTON POLICE DEPARTMENT (2004–2009)

In 2007, 38-year-old Officer Edgardo Rodriguez "pleaded guilty to a six-count indictment that charged him with conspiracy to distribute anabolic steroids, distribution of anabolic steroids, three counts of

---

[1]See Buser (2007); Johnson (2013); Lane (2013); McLamb (2011); Pack (2014).

perjury before a federal grand jury, and obstruction of justice" (Abel, 2007). The US Attorney made it clear that this officer's behavior was intolerable (Abel, 2007):

"The response to false testimony by a police officer should be swift and unequivocal," US Attorney Michael J. Sullivan said in a written statement. "There is no place in our system of justice for a law enforcement officer to lie to a grand jury, or to take any other action to obstruct the investigation of vitally important matters."

...Between February and June 2006, Rodriguez conspired with former Boston police officer Roberto Pulido to distribute and to possess with intent to distribute anabolic steroids, which are a controlled substance under federal law, prosecutors said. They said investigators intercepted Pulido's phone calls with Rodriguez and others.

In 2003, Rodriguez distributed steroids to another officer, who returned the steroids to him, prosecutors said. On Oct. 5, 2006, after the arrests of Pulido and former officers Nelson Carrasquillo and Carlos Pizarro, Rodriguez appeared before a federal grand jury investigating police corruption. In his testimony, Rodriguez made false statements under oath about steroid use and distribution by other officers, prosecutors said.

Rodriguez faces a maximum sentence of five years in prison on each of the conspiracy, distribution, and three perjury charges. He faces 10 years in prison on the charge of obstruction of justice.

In 2008, another Boston police officer, Kevin Guy, tested positive for steroids. He received a 45-day suspension.

In 2009, the Boston Police Department suffered its biggest public steroid abuse scandal of all, involving 11 officers over a period of at least 8 years, as reported in Cramer (2009):

Eleven Boston police officers have been disciplined for their role in a steroids scandal that humiliated the department, forced officials to tighten their drug policies, and resulted in prison time for four patrolmen.

The disciplined officers, seven of whom admitted to using steroids at some point in their careers, received punishments ranging from a written reprimand to a 45-day suspension without pay. But none of the officers were fired and none will face criminal charges, Boston Police Commissioner Edward F. Davis said today.

"I am disappointed with the actions of the officers disciplined in this matter," he said during a news conference at police headquarters. "We remain steadfast in our dedication to preserving the integrity of our department by taking every measure to prevent and when necessary uncover officer misconduct."

The punishments were the culmination of an investigation that began in August 2006 soon after the FBI arrested Officer Roberto "Kiko" Pulido for trying to traffic cocaine. Pulido, a steroid user, would guard parties hosted by a convicted drug dealer at an after-hours club in Hyde Park called the "Boom Boom Room."

Pulido was sentenced to 26 years in prison. Two other officers, Nelson Carrasquillo and Carlos Pizarro, received sentences of 18 years and 13 years, respectively.

Two of the 11 officers were disciplined for going to the club in uniform and while they were on duty. The club sat above an auto body shop on Factory Street, where prostitutes and dancers mingled with police and where alcohol and drugs were readily available.

Acting US Attorney Michael Loucks said today that the federal investigation regarding Pulido and steroids use in the Boston Police Department has been closed. Pulido pleaded guilty in November 2008 to charges that he conspired to traffic cocaine and heroin from Western Massachusetts to Jamaica Plain. He was sentenced to 26 years in federal prison.

The disciplinary action against the officers ends one of the most embarrassing chapters in the department's history, but questions linger about how effective the police can be in controlling steroid use in the department, considering how difficult it is to test for the drug. Unlike other narcotics, steroid testing is much more expensive and results from taking hair samples can be less accurate, resulting in false positives.

Davis said that since the federal investigation has begun, the department has begun training supervisors to spot signs of substance abuse, especially steroids. Supervisors are also going through "integrity training," which reviews the department's ethics, like reporting wrongdoing by other officers.

Officers and recruits must take courses that teach the health risks of using anabolic steroids. New recruits will be tested for steroids.

The department also negotiated testing officers who violated the drug abuse policy for their entire careers, instead of just a three-year period. "There is an emerging trend of steroid use in law enforcement that we're monitoring very closely," Davis said.

The disciplined officers included:

• Steven Gil, a 39-year-old patrolman, who was suspended for three days for failing to notify the department about other officers' steroid use.
• Kenneth Gaines, a 44-year-old detective, who was suspended for 30 days for using steroids in 2004.
• Joseph Marrero, a 34-year-old detective, who was suspended for 30 days for using steroids in 2002.
• Richard Medina, a 36-year-old patrolman, who was suspended for 15 days for using steroids in 2001.
• Martin Harrison, a 37-year-old patrolman, who was suspended for 30 days for using steroids in 2005 and 2006.
• David Juba, a 35-year-old patrolman, who was suspended for 45 days for using steroids in 2006, then lying about it. He also was punished for going to the Boom Boom Room twice while he was on duty and in uniform.
• Luke Holbrook, a 36-year-old patrolman, who was suspended for 40 days for using steroids in 2006, then lying about it.

- Timothy Hancock, a 41-year-old patrolman, who was disciplined for 30 days for using steroids in 2004.
- Joseph Dominguez, a 37-year-old patrolman, who was disciplined for three days for going to the Boom Boom Room while he was on duty and in uniform.
- Carl Shorter, a 41-year-old patrolman, was disciplined the same amount of time for the same violation.
- Nichole Tyler, a 39-year-old patrolwoman, received a written reprimand for leaving her assigned post to drop off her partner at the club.

All of the officers accused of steroid use will be subject to drug tests for their entire careers.

Illegal steroid use is serious misconduct evidencing complicity with and participation in criminal activity. This is demonstrated by the nature of the behavior itself as well as the circumstances specific to this case. However, the 11 officers named are all still on the job and suffered no criminal sanctions. This would seem to make it impossible for them to be effective in their public safety duties, that is if their misconduct is disclosed in any case where they are expected to give sworn testimony.

7.2 NEW YORK CITY DEPARTMENT (2007–2008)

In late 2007, a scandal was made public regarding anabolic steroid abuse within the ranks of the New York City Police Department. The results of the investigation were hidden, those involved kept quiet, and the known consequences for those responsible were all but nonexistent. As reported in Gardiner (2007):

...the Brooklyn District Attorney's Office knows of 29 cops and at least 10 NYPD civilian employees—all well under the age of 60—who have received prescriptions for hypogonadism. The treatment for it just happens to be steroids.
...when the story first broke in October, NYPD officials repeatedly said that only six officers were believed to be involved. Spokesman Paul Browne has maintained that none of the cops were selling steroids and none will be arrested, though they may face departmental discipline.
...people close to the probe, speaking on the condition of anonymity, say that in the probe of cops' steroid use, investigators from the State Department of Health have given the D.A. almost a dozen boxes of records gathered during three raids at Lowen's Pharmacy in Brooklyn. Officials have also seized millions of dollars of human growth hormone (HGH) and steroids from that Bay Ridge pharmacy. The most recent raid was on December 3. Hynes won't comment other than to confirm that there is an investigation.

But sources tell the Voice that one officer bought more than $25,000 worth of steroids in a year, an amount that is impossible to claim as personal use. Cops found to have filed false insurance claims or sold steroids could face the possibility of criminal charges, as could cops who've received prescriptions for steroids unless it's determined that they're for legitimate medical reasons.

But that's just the steroids angle of the investigation. Investigators are still sifting through 4,000 to 5,000 HGH prescriptions filled at Lowen's in the past 18 months. Dr. Harry Fisch, a professor of clinical urology at Columbia University, says there are only two legitimate medical reasons for an adult to be prescribed HGH: to offset the loss of body mass and muscle for people in the advanced stages of AIDS and to treat a rare pituitary condition.

Those HGH records at Lowen's could open up a Pandora's box in the largest police department in the nation. NYPD officials have kept a lid on the steroids angle of the probe—amid grumbling in the ranks. The fact that the two highest-ranking officers caught up in the probe so far—two deputy chiefs, Mike Marino, executive officer of the Brooklyn North patrol, and Jack Trabitz, head of the property-clerk division—were not suspended and appear to have been cleared despite admitting they received prescriptions for testosterone has Patrick Lynch, president of the rank-and-file patrol officers' union, crying "favoritism." Trabitz didn't return calls seeking comment. One cop has told the Voice that Trabitz, who is in his 50s, "looks like he could be a running back in the NFL, he's that big." Marino came forward after his name was leaked to the press. Reportedly, however, he was cleared after being questioned by the Internal Affairs Bureau, which found his prescription to be legitimate.

Marino tells the Voice that he can't comment "because there's some litigation going on around this right now." John Driscoll, outgoing president of the Captains Endowment Association, the union for those with the rank of captain and above, says that that Marino and Trabitz not only voluntarily talked with IAB investigators but also took drug tests and passed them. At this point, Driscoll says, they are "accused of nothing."

Previously published reports didn't detail what Marino's supposed ailment was, but law enforcement sources tell the Voice that Marino told IAB investigators that in addition to being treated for a low sex drive, he had been prescribed the drug to lose weight.

"That's not a legitimate reason for using anabolic steroids," says Dr. Gary Wadler, author of Drugs and the Athlete and a member of the World Anti-Doping Agency's Prohibited List and Methods Committee. "It's not a weight-reducing drug."

In 2001, Marino's remarkable bodybuilding was featured in the New York magazine article "Captain Midnight." After Marino got pushed around by street toughs as a skinny rookie in Harlem, the article noted, the cop "bulked up from 152 pounds to 190, had eighteen-inch arms, and could bench-press 350 pounds." It goes on to describe how Marino, who admitted that weightlifting changed his temperament, knocked out many a criminal and cop and how his wife divorced him, saying, "You're not the man I married, mentally or physically."

Former NYPD captain Eric Adams, once the leader of an organization of NYPD's black cops and now a state senator, says that "like baseball, in order to get a handle on how widespread the problem is, the NYPD should include steroids" in its random drug tests. When he was on the job, Adams says, he didn't see anyone taking steroids. And he adds that there was no discussion of steroids among the cops with whom he worked out. There were suspicions, however. "You'd be in the gym and sometimes you know a guy is doing them," he says. "You can tell when a guy is on 'roids: He'd be very aggressive, have mood swings. But there was nothing rampant."

A Manhattan cop previously stationed in Brooklyn contends that, for practical reasons, "relatively few" are willing to cross the line to do steroids. Many are obsessed with working out, not with doughnuts. "Contrary to popular belief," he says, "cops are more buffy than most people think." Creatine and other legal workout supplements are extremely popular among cops, he says, but obtaining steroids is more involved and risky, and most cops are paranoid of doing anything that will jeopardize their 20-and-out pensions.

Adams agrees that many cops try to beef up by legal means. "In law enforcement, everyone wants to be as buff as possible," Adams says. "Everyone wants to exercise as much as possible." Or maybe more than just work out—especially after they leave the gym. People weaning themselves from steroids, says Wadler, often "have high incidence of depression and even suicide"—and still have those department-issued weapons strapped to their hips.

"They're playing Russian roulette with their health," he says. "Of course, in a cop you worry about 'roid rage more than with the average person. Steroids can make people more aggressive—severely aggressive—and you don't want a severely aggressive person being put in a position where they have their finger on the trigger of a gun."

Or with their hands on a broom handle. Cops are fully aware that during their colleague Justin Volpe's trial for the 1999 torture of Abner Louima, during which a broom handle was shoved up the ass of the immigrant in the 70th Precinct bathroom, a Volpe family confidant said the cop should have claimed temporary insanity caused by 'roid rage.

The Manhattan cop tells the Voice that "you automatically think of Volpe and how he lost it." But he says cops generally don't discuss the dangers of 'roid rage. "Most cops I've talked with don't give a shit about that," he says. "They're more concerned that the chief [Marino] got away with it and the cops are getting jammed up."

...According to law-enforcement sources, the NYPD has had to order the cops suspected of using to undergo special tests because the standard NYPD urinalysis exam doesn't detect steroids. There is no known test for HGH.

According to sources, six cops have tested positive for steroids: Sergeant Ray Cotton of Patrol Borough South and his officer-driver Vaughn Etienne; Sergeant Manny DaSilva of the 61st Precinct; and officers James Prinzo of the 60th Precinct, Frank Perna of the 68th Precinct, and Tab Haynes of the Staten Island task force. All but Haynes are Brooklyn cops. All six were suspended and then placed on modified duty. Their lawyers have declined comment.

Investigators are still trying to determine how the cops allegedly implicated in the Lowen's probe got turned on to the pharmacy in the first place. And cops aren't the only ones facing a probe. So far, 19 New York City firefighters have been found to have received prescriptions for steroids and/or HGH that were filled at Lowen's, sources say.

FDNY spokesman Frank Gribbon says the department has not been notified that any firefighters had obtained prescriptions for steroids related to the investigation that revolves around Lowen's. Like the NYPD, the FDNY doesn't include steroids in its random drug tests.

In the past year, Lowen's has become what law-enforcement officials believe was one of the busiest steroid and HGH outlets in the country. Those involved in this alleged 'roid mill include a Beverly Hills chiropractor with a degree in hypnotism, a mob associate/movie producer named Julius "Jules" Nasso who did time for extorting actor Steven Seagal, a former pump-and-dump stock operator who owns a gym, and a Staten Island doctor who had an office in what was known as the "Fountain of Youth Building," across the street from a cemetery.

...Investigators subsequently found that over the past 18 months, of the approximately 15,000 "Schedule II" prescriptions (drugs such as oxycodone, Ritalin, and Dexedrine) that Lowen's filled, a huge number of them—9,300—were for steroids, law-enforcement sources tell the Voice. That's on top of 4,000 to 5,000 prescriptions the drug store has filled during that time period for HGH. Given those figures, sources say, Lowen's could have been doing as much as $30 million a year in steroid and HGH business.

...In addition to the pharmacy's connection with Nasso, it is also associated with New York Anti-Aging & Wellness Medical Services, a Staten Island hormone-therapy clinic also at the center of the steroid probe. The principals in that venture include osteopath Richard Lucente and John Amato, a/k/a "Flames," who owns several Dolphin Fitness Center gyms. Amato did 15 months in prison and was ordered to make $182,000 in restitution for a pump-and-dump stock scam in 2000 involving a company supposedly operating health clubs. [Lowen's owner John] Rossi's son-in-law, Edward Letendre, is also a partner in the clinic and a vice president of Lowen's.

The Staten Island clinic was located in the small, redbrick "Fountain of Youth Building" across the street from St. Peter's Cemetery. In a small office on the lower level of that building, Lucente also operated the Life Longevity Center. The office was raided several months ago and appears to have since been vacated. Investigators have found that Lucente wrote more than 2,000 of the 9,300 steroid prescriptions filled at Lowen's over the past 18 months, according to law-enforcement sources.

Lucente tells the Voice that the prescriptions he wrote for the NYPD cops were legitimate. He says that he has some renown in the specialty of hormone replacement and that the officers he saw, most of whom were in their 30s and 40s, were in fact suffering from low testosterone. It's not unusual for a group of men in that age range to suffer from hypogonadism, he says. Lucente denies that the cops were using the testosterone creams and injectible *drug to build muscles. (A doctor tells the* Voice *that it's highly unlikely that a group of relatively young cops would be suffering from hypogonadism. In addition, chronic steroid use has been known to eventually cause the users' testicles to shrink and shrivel.)*

Lucente contends that the focus of the investigation is solely on Lowen's, not on him. "I haven't been charged with anything, nor do I expect to be," says Lucente. When asked if he was cooperating with authorities in the probe, Lucente declined comment.

In 2007, Lowen's owner John Rossi committed suicide before the investigation into his criminal behavior could be concluded. However, Doctor Richard Lucente of Staten Island was arrested and charged with crimes related to his involvement in the scandal—for selling out his medical license to profit from steroid addicts. In 2010, he pled guilty and negotiated a no time deal with prosecutors, as reported in Schifrel (2010):

[Lucente] was sentenced Wednesday to five years' probation and 200 hours of community service, and promised to give up practicing medicine for two years.

The sentencing marked the end of a wide-ranging, highly publicized steroid probe that ended with no one going to prison.

It is important to note that despite the seriousness of the misconduct involved, and its impact on officer integrity and overall fitness for duty, there were no criminal consequences meted out to any of the public safety officers involved. However, some were disciplined administratively. This means that all of the public safety employees involved kept their jobs, and are not necessarily subject to ongoing testing for anabolic steroid abuse despite their known history.

7.3 PHILADELPHIA POLICE DEPARTMENT (2011)

In 2011, three members of the Philadelphia Police Department were charged with several others for operating an illegal steroid trafficking ring. This included Det. Keith Gidelson and his wife, Kirsten. As reported in a press release by the US Attorney's Office (Hartman, 2013):

Keith Gidelson, 36, a former Philadelphia Police Detective, was sentenced today to 4 years in prison for operating anabolic steroid and human growth hormone ("HGH") distribution organization in Philadelphia and throughout the United States. His wife, Kirsten Gidelson, was sentenced to three years probation, with the first year on home confinement, and a $100 special assessment, for her participation in the conspiracy. Gidelson acquired steroids *from foreign suppliers and then sold these steroids to his co-conspirators who distributed the drugs to their own customers. He pleaded guilty October 9, 2012, to conspiracy to distribute anabolic steroids and 16 counts of possession with intent to distribute anabolic steroids. In addition to the prison term, U.S. District Court Judge Paul S. Diamond ordered Gidelson to pay a $25,000 fine and ordered three years of supervised release.*

Gidelson received monthly shipments of anabolic steroids and HGH from suppliers in Europe and China. One supplier shipped the steroids to California where defendant Robert Walters re-packaged them for shipment to Gidelson. Another supplier shipped orders of steroids to a mailbox that Gidelson had rented at a UPS store. Gidelson and his wife stored and packaged steroids and HGH at their home in Philadelphia. The couple met with drug customers, including defendants Michael Barclay, Keith Ebner, Jeffrey Filoon, Christian Kowalko, Joel Levin, Luke Lors, Joseph McIntyre, George Sambuca, William Schiavo, and Vaidotas Verikas, at their home and at Philadelphia-area fitness clubs, to distribute anabolic steroids and HGH in various quantities.

Gidelson also distributed steroids to customers throughout the United States that he met through online weightlifting chat rooms on websites including: Steroids.com; Inject.com; Isteroids.com; and Bodybuilding.com. Gidelson also allegedly used the electronic mail service yahoo.com, and the encrypted email services hushmail.com and safemail.com to place orders and communicate with his foreign suppliers.

The case was investigated by the Drug Enforcement Administration, the Federal Bureau of Investigation, the Philadelphia Police Department, and the United States Postal Inspection Service. It was prosecuted by Assistant United States Attorney David L. Axelrod.

Gidelson was on disability leave when his criminal activity was uncovered, as reported in Martin (2012):

Gidelson was still on the city payroll but on disability leave in August 2010 when a confidential source told authorities he bought steroids from the detective, Assistant U.S. Attorney David L. Axelrod told the judge.

In the ensuing months, investigators from the Drug Enforcement Administration and the Postal Service launched surveillance of Gidelson's home, tapped his cellphone, and monitored his mail.

...Gidelson told the judge that he became addicted to painkillers after suffering a serious injury in an on-the-job car crash in 2006. He has since been treated for the pill addiction, post-traumatic stress disorder, anxiety, and other ailments. [His attorney] said after the hearing that the loss of his job, the addiction to painkillers, and other personal problems fueled Gidelson's slide into drug sales.

Officer Joseph McIntyre and Officer George Sambuca, also of Philadelphia Police Department, pled guilty to their involvement in the same steroid trafficking ring. All three were sentenced in 2013.

7.4 NEW JERSEY (2010–2011)

Perhaps one of the largest documented steroid abuse scandals in public safety was centered in New Jersey, extending across multiple police and fire departments in multiple states. As reported in Brittain and Mueller (2010):

Reported in Brittain and Mueller (2010): "Rafael Galan, an officer in the Passaic County Sheriff's Department, received anabolic steroids from Jersey City physician Joseph Colao. Galan, shown posing in 2006 for a calendar shoot, faced a criminal charge of official misconduct for allegedly tipping off the subject of a drug investigation." The charge was layer dropped, and Officer Galan was reinstated. In 2014, however, Galan was arrested, and this time the charges were more serious (Augenstein, 2014): "Rafael Galan, a 23-year veteran of the sheriff's office, was charged with official misconduct, conspiracy to receive stolen property, receiving stolen property, unlawful alteration to motor vehicle identification numbers, tampering with public records, and misrepresentation in motor-vehicle records, said Camelia Valdes, the Passaic County prosecutor."

A seven-month Star-Ledger *investigation drawing on prescription records, court documents and detailed interviews with the physician's employees shows [Dr. Joseph] Colao ran a thriving illegal drug enterprise that supplied anabolic steroids and human growth hormone to hundreds of law enforcement officers and firefighters throughout New Jersey.*

From a seemingly above-board practice in Jersey City, Colao frequently broke the law and his own oath by faking medical diagnoses to justify his prescriptions for the drugs, the investigation shows.

Many of the officers and firefighters willingly took part in the ruse, finding Colao provided an easy way to obtain tightly regulated substances that are illegal without a valid prescription, the investigation found.

Others were persuaded by the physician's polished sales pitch, one that glossed over the risks and legal realities, the newspaper found. A small percentage may have legitimately needed the drugs to treat uncommon medical conditions.

In most cases, if not all, they used their government health plans to pay for the substances. Evidence gathered by The Star-Ledger *suggests the total cost to taxpayers reaches into the millions of dollars.*

In just over a year, records show, at least 248 officers and firefighters from 53 agencies used Colao's fraudulent practice to obtain muscle-building drugs, some of which have been linked to increased aggression, confusion and reckless behavior.

Six of those patients—four police officers and two corrections officers— were named in lawsuits alleging excessive force or civil rights violations around the time they received drugs from him or shortly afterward.

Others have been arrested, fired or suspended for off-duty infractions that include allegations of assault, domestic abuse, harassment and drug possession. One patient was left nearly paralyzed after suffering a stroke his doctor attributed to growth hormone prescribed by Colao.

For many in the physician's care, use of the drugs apparently didn't end with Colao's death.

They instead sought other doctors who specialize in prescribing growth hormone or testosterone, an anabolic steroid, according to patients, legal documents and the doctors themselves. The physicians have not been accused of wrongdoing.

In 2007, Dr. Joseph Colao collapsed from heart failure (hardening of the arteries) in his Jersey City apartment at the age of 45.

Subsequent to this scandal, the Attorney General's Office for the State of New Jersey acknowledged the problem in a serious and public fashion. It prepared a report detailing how anabolic steroids are listed as Schedule III Controlled Substances with related criminal penalties for abuse, along with suggestions for reforming law enforcement to curb their abuse (AGSSG, 2011). Although the impact of this report on local law enforcement agencies is unproved as of this writing, the gesture is not an empty one. The report exists as an important benchmark, and guidepost, with respect to the handling of these kinds of scandals in public safety.

7.5 THE PHILLIP WILBUR CASE: COBB COUNTY, GEORGIA (2013–PRESENT)

A number of news outlets covered this scandal, which is ongoing, for a period of time during 2013. As a result, many of the details are quite public. This includes the identities of some of those involved. A helpful summary is reported in Wiley (2013):

Darnell
Musgrove
terminated

E. A.
Meadors
resigned

Vaughn D.
Zellers
suspended

Jody
Cochran
suspended

These individuals suffered various levels of consequences for essentially the same criminal misconduct: buying and abusing illegal anabolic steroids, and then lying about it to investigators.

One Cobb firefighter is without a job and another two are suspended without pay following an investigation into alleged use and distribution of steroids by county firefighters and one police officer.

The substances in question are anabolic steroids, including the male hormone testosterone and deca-durabolin, which are illegal to use without a prescription. . .

The investigation began the week of May 20 when officials were told by the Marietta Cobb Smyrna Narcotics Unit that a county employee may have illegally used steroids. Originally targeting one former firefighter accused of using steroids in 2010, the investigation grew following claims that other firefighters and a police officer could be involved. . .

A 27-year county firefighter with no previous discipline problems was terminated Monday after admitting he sold two vials of steroids in late December and early January. Darnell Musgrove of Dallas initially told internal affairs investigators he used steroids about seven or eight years ago. But after agents said they had evidence of recent use, he changed his story, according to a memo obtained by the MDJ.

He admitted to using prescription and non-prescription steroids alongside each other and handed over two bottles of steroids he obtained illegally to investigators, according to the memo. He also said he resold bottles of testosterone.

"The two employees you identified have denied that you sold them illegal testosterone, although one admits that he met you, discussed a possible transaction, but then decided not to make the purchase," said Fire Chief Sam Heaton in a letter to Musgrove. Musgrove is also accused of discussing the investigation after being told not to by internal affairs and refusing to submit to a polygraph test. "It's also clear from your statements and actions that you have not seen that such conduct is a problem," Heaton said in the letter. "Neither does it appear that you have taken any steps to get help for your reliance upon an illegal substance.". . .

Firefighter Vaughn Zellers of Acworth and Engineer Jody Cochran of Douglasville have been suspended after admitting to using steroids.

> *Zellers allegedly lied during his first interview with internal affairs and then admitted to purchasing three or four vials of illegal steroids from a former fire department employee in 2008. He also admitted, according to a county memo, to meeting with a current fire employee to look at some vials of testosterone but denied making purchases. . ..*
>
> *"While it does not appear that your illegal use of steroids resulted in behavior putting others at risk, I believe that your actions did at the time show a disregard for the responsibility you hold for the safety of others," Heaton said in a memo dated Aug. 9. . .*
>
> *His service was also considered, Heaton said. The 15-year firefighter served in the U.S. Marines, a Woodstock police officer, and a firefighter, paramedic and hazardous materials technician with the Cobb Fire Department. . .*
>
> *Cochran, a 25-year firefighter, has been suspended for three days without pay and told investigators he did not know he was using testosterone illegally because he had a prescription for it though he did not purchase it from a pharmacy. He admitted to obtaining two vials from a former fire employee. "I did not really see anything wrong with it. I didn't know if it was illegal or not (because) I had a prescription for it," Cochran said, according to a memo dated Aug. 9. "I didn't know there was a law if you got to get it straight from a pharmacy."*
>
> *Heaton found that problematic. "Your paramedic position requires you to administer various medications through medical control approval, yet you consistently advised the (internal affairs) investigators you 'saw nothing wrong with it' when referring to the purchase of an illegal controlled substance," Heaton said in the Aug. 9 memo.*

Both authors have participated directly, and indirectly, in this investigation. It was initiated by a complaint filed by one of the authors (Crowder) with the drug task force regarding fireman Phillip Wilbur. Wilbur was known to be abusing and dealing anabolic steroids, as well as possessing them in large quantities. The lessons learned from this investigation with respect to the varied responses of law enforcement agencies and the judiciary are, in fact, the primary impetus for this current reference manual.

7.5.1 Meadors

Former Cobb County police officer Eric Meadors admitted to the purchase and use of illegal anabolic steroids. This confession came after he tested positive for illegal drug use during an internal affairs investigation.[2] Meadors admitted to buying steroids when he worked in a gym before becoming a police officer, and admitted to purchasing steroids from a firefighter who worked for the same county where

[2]Eric Meadors is a former student of both authors.

Meadors was employed. The Internal Affairs Report notes, "Officer Meadors said he purchased three vials of testosterone Cypionate (Deca) for approximately $100.00 per vial from Phillip Wilbur" (Cobb County Department of Public Safety Internal Affairs, 2013b, synopsis, p. 1). To be clear, Phillip Wilbur was the firefighter that Meadors admitted buying steroids from.

The Internal Affairs Report continues, "Officer Meadors admitted to buying, possessing, and using illegal anabolic steroids prior to being employed which he failed to disclose on his application for employment. Officer Meadors also purchased, possessed, and used illegal injectable steroids while employed as a Cobb County Police officer" (Cobb County Department of Public Safety Internal Affairs, 2013b, synopsis, p. 3).

When asked about other police officers in the department using steroids, Meadors offered, "I don't have proof but, I mean there's people I suspect. I mean, you can look at any of the guys that are more than above average in their PT tests and have substantial muscle...I mean it's...I'm only 192 pounds so it's not like I'm some huge guy but, again, I don't have...I have suspicions of certain people who may or may not be using but that's not here nor there. I've never discussed it with anybody..." (Cobb County Department of Public Safety Internal Affairs, 2013b, p. 31).

Near the end of former Officer Meadors' testimony, he also stated, "...I just apologize that I wasn't forthcoming with my use of it since I've been a police officer because again... human nature...I just...it's kind of like a, I know what happens from here so...."(Cobb County Department of Public Safety Internal Affairs, 2013b, p. 31). Officer Meadors knew he had lied on his job application, admitted to illegally buying and using anabolic steroids, and was well aware his law enforcement career was over.

Despite this acknowledgment, Officer Meadors hedged on the issue of Boldenone: "On June 28, 2013, Internal Affairs received the drug screen results for Ofc. Meadors which indicated he tested positive for the drug Boldenone which is an injectable steroid used in the growth or repair of muscles in a horse or other animal" (Georgia Peace Officers Standards and Training Council, Investigative Report 0078741013, page not numbered). With these results in hand, the internal affairs investigator asked Officer Meadors if he had ever heard of the drug Boldenone, to which Meadors responded, "Only after I researched it after I was contacted by the drug lab..." (Cobb County Department of Public Safety Internal Affairs, 2013b, p. 57). One does not accidentally inject the drug Equipoise (Boldenone).

With respect to Officer Meador's motivation for abusing illegal anabolic steroids, he admits, "...given our profession, some guys that, you know, use those types of substances that maintain a level of fitness or, you know, ability to do their job..." (Cobb County Department of Public Safety Internal Affairs, 2013b, p. 30). However, Meadors vacillates between "...my actions are inexcusable..." to "I just was doing what I thought I needed to do to maintain my, my edge..." (Cobb County Department of Public Safety Internal Affairs, 2013b, p. 63).

Ultimately, the Internal Affairs investigation into Officer Eric Meadors revealed sustained allegations of violation of rules (Code of Conduct 1.01), unbecoming conduct (Code of Conduct 1.02), conformance to laws (Code of Conduct 1.04), and use of alcohol, drugs, or narcotics (Code of Conduct 1.14). Subsequent to his drug test and interview with Internal Affairs, Meadors did not hesitate to resign from the department before being fired.

7.5.2 Musgrove

Firefighter Darnell Musgrove admitted to buying his illegal anabolic steroids from Phillip Wilbur. When asked if he understood whether buying illegal drugs was in fact illegal, Musgrove responded, "Correct" (Cobb County Department of Public Safety Internal Affairs, 2013a, p. 148). Further, Musgrove admitted to selling anabolic steroids to firefighters Rick Bennett and Charlie Zellers (Cobb County Department of Public Safety Internal Affairs, 2013a, p. 150). When asked how rampant the use of anabolic steroids was in the fire department, Musgrove responded, "I think it's all over the nation, actually public service" (Cobb County Department of Public Safety Internal Affairs, 2013a, p. 164).

When asked "why did you find it necessary to buy illegal steroids and inject those?" Firefighter Musgrove responded, "The thought process is um, it...it helps ah, ah, sexual performance..." (Cobb County Department of Public Safety Internal Affairs, 2013a, p. 148).

When asked would you classify that there is an issue, a problem (use of illegal anabolic steroids) with the Cobb County Fire Department, Musgrove responded, "I would think so" (Cobb County Department of Public Safety Internal Affairs, 2013a, p. 165).

7.5.3 Zellers

In the first interview with Firefighter Vaughn "Charlie" Zellers, "there had been some untruths and some flat out deception," so a second interview was conducted (Cobb County Department of Public Safety Internal Affairs, 2013a, p. 531). Zellers motivation for buying and using illegal anabolic steroids was quickly established, "...I wanted to get back in shape and start to date again and, uh, I started working out and then, um, I started to take some steroids to get in better shape..." (Cobb County Department of Public Safety Internal Affairs, 2013a, p. 534).

Zellers admitted to using the same firefighter drug dealer, Phillip Wilbur, as his supplier of testosterone cypionate (Cobb County Department of Public Safety Internal Affairs, 2013a, p. 534). He admitted to paying Wilbur for three or four bottles at $50–$60 dollars per bottle (Cobb County Department of Public Safety Internal Affairs, 2013a, p. 535). However, later in the interview, a crying Zellers admitted to more buys from Wilbur (Cobb County Department of Public Safety Internal Affairs, 2013a, p. 539). Zellers denied buying from Firefighter Musgrove, but Musgrove was clear in his testimony that he sold to Zellers. Zellers admits, "...I've taken it, I've bought it, I've done it..." (Cobb County Department of Public Safety Internal Affairs, 2013a, p. 550).

Zellers second interview ended with a number of revelations. Zellers named Eric (Meadors), a guy named Will (at the police department), Frank Adams at the fire department, then he dropped the bomb. When asked, "How widespread with the fire department and uh, police department do you think this is?" Zellers responded, "If you...if you went through everyone's personnel files and found out who is on testosterone, I would guess that 90 percent of them are abusing" (Cobb County Department of Public Safety Internal Affairs, 2013a, p. 553). When asked, "Does it make that big a difference?" Zellers stated, "Oh yeah. I mean you feel like you're 20 years old and can do anything. And you look good" (Cobb County Department of Public Safety Internal Affairs, 2013a, p. 554). "I felt like I could lift a house" (Cobb County Department of Public Safety Internal Affairs, 2013a, p. 555).

7.5.4 Nemeth

Seven-year veteran of the fire department, Craig A. Nemeth quickly admitted his use of illegal steroids to Internal Affairs investigators (Cobb County Department of Public Safety Internal Affairs, 2013a, p. 242). He named Phillip Wilbur as the person he got the illegal drugs from (Cobb County Department of Public Safety Internal Affairs, 2013a, p. 243). He admitted paying Wilbur $40.00 for the drugs the first time, and then purchasing multiple vials of steroids thereafter (Cobb County Department of Public Safety Internal Affairs, 2013a, p. 258).

Nemeth acknowledged that these drug deals took place at Wilbur's home, possibly when Wilbur's wife and children were at home (Cobb County Department of Public Safety Internal Affairs, 2013a, pp. 243–244, 255). Wilbur also provided the needles for Nemeth to inject himself (Cobb County Department of Public Safety Internal Affairs, 2013a, pp. 247, 251). Nemeth further reported that his drug dealer, Phillip Wilbur, told him, "There are people...there's ...there's more people than you would think that are taking it" (Cobb County Department of Public Safety Internal Affairs, 2013a, p. 255).

Nemeth also admitted that he sold some of the steroids back to Wilbur, again at the Wilbur home where he lived with his wife and children (Cobb County Department of Public Safety Internal Affairs, 2013a, p. 263).

Craig Nemeth did apologize to Internal Affairs investigators, offering "...I want to add is just I'm sorry" (Cobb County Department of Public Safety Internal Affairs, 2013a, p. 262). However, it seems likely that he was sorry he was caught. Certainly, his illegal drug use was not showing signs of abating prior to their efforts.

7.5.5 Cochran

When Firefighter Jody Cochran was interviewed, he quickly explained that he was on prescribed drugs. He further explained that he purchased steroids from an Internet site, "TradeKey" (Cobb County

Department of Public Safety Internal Affairs Investigation, 2013a, p. 435). However, he admitted that Phillip Wilbur also gave him steroids (Cobb County Department of Public Safety Internal Affairs, 2013a, p. 436) and needles to use (Cobb County Department of Public Safety Internal Affairs, 2013a, p. 440).

When Cochran was asked if he understood that taking a vial of steroids (testosterone) was illegal, Cochran responded, "Yeah" (Cobb County Department of Public Safety Internal Affairs, 2013a, p. 442).

Cochran eventually admitted to purchasing a vial, or maybe two, from Wilbur (Cobb County Department of Public Safety Internal Affairs, 2013a, page 448). He also admitted to knowledge that Wilbur was selling to a number of firemen throughout the county (Cobb County Department of Public Safety Internal Affairs, 2013a, p. 542).

Firefighter Cochran also eventually admitted to making drug transactions at Wilbur's home (Cobb County Department of Public Safety Internal Affairs, 2013a, p. 452) and at a park while Wilbur's young son was there playing in a football game (Cobb County Department of Public Safety Internal Affairs, 2013a, pp. 456, 461).

When polygraphed about his illegal steroid usage, Cochran attempted to manipulate the results in order to beat the test. Investigators reported that: "It is the belief and opinion that Jody had knowingly and purposefully engaged in an attempt to beat the test by manipulating his breathing and excessive foot movements" (Cobb County Department of Public Safety Internal Affairs, 2013a, p. 520).

7.5.6 Bennett

When asked about subordinate misconduct involving steroids, and his duty of care, Fire Lieutenant Rick Bennett replied, "I have a responsibility to report it if I know it. I don't have a responsibility to dig for it" (Cobb County Department of Public Safety, 2013a, p. 716). Ignorance is bliss; especially if you are a past steroid user as Bennett later admits.

Bennett ignored accusations and rumors that Phillip Wilbur used steroids (Cobb County Department of Public Safety Internal Affairs, 2013a, p. 202). Yet, when Rick Bennett was asked if he knew who offered his name up as having taken testosterone cypionate Bennett quickly replied, "I would be willing to bet that it would probably be um, ah, Phillip Wilbur cause he's the only person that I know whose name has been specifically linked to steroids and his name is the only name that I known that...I say I've known. It's been talk that when he was at ah, Smyrna Fire Department that they found his car full of um, illegal steroids" (Cobb County Department of Public Safety Internal Affairs, 2013a, p. 700).

When Lieutenant Bennett learned that it was firefighter Musgrove that reported he sold steroids to him, Bennett denied it. Bennett did admit, "Ever ingested oral steroid? In high school. In high school" (Cobb County Department of Public Safety Internal Affairs, 2013a, pp. 216, 217). Bennett admitted to taking Dianabol (methandrostenolone) as early as the ninth grade (Cobb County Department of Public Safety Internal Affairs, 2013a, p. 217).

Multiple documents in the case file on Bennett demonstrate that he failed the polygraph test administered to him which included the questions: "Since you've been employed by Cobb County have you used any type of illegal steroids? Since you've been employed by Cobb County have you sold any type of illegal steroids? Since you've been employed with Cobb County have you purchased any type of illegal steroids?" (Cobb County Department of Public Safety Internal Affairs, 2013a, pp. 710, 711).

The polygraph examiner concluded: "After conducting three polygraph charts utilizing a Modified General Question Technique, it is the opinion of this examiner that there were SIGNIFICANT PHYSIOLOGICAL RESPONSES (capitalized in original documents) present at the above listed questions" (Cobb County Department of Public Safety Internal Affairs, 2013a, pp. 421, 711).

7.5.7 Wilbur

There can be no mistake that firefighter Phillip Wilbur has been established as the illegal anabolic steroid dealer in the cases provided above.

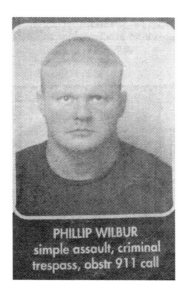

Published mugshot of Phillip Wilbur from an incident in April of 2011. He was able to get his record expunged when the prosecutor dropped the case. He has since been rearrested for forgery first degree (felony). However, no police agency is willing to arrest him for drug dealing, and no related charges have been brought against him by any prosecutors despite a mountain of evidence and admissions.

As reported in the Internal Affair investigation, an examination of Wilbur's behavior reveals sustained allegations of unbecoming conduct, failure in conformance to laws, use of drugs, and false testimony under oath (Cobb County Department of Public Safety Internal Affairs, 2011, p. 1).

Firefighter Wilbur first came to the attention of internal affairs investigators after two arrests: one arrest for multiple charges in a domestic violence incident and another arrest for theft. In his second interview with investigators (May 5, 2011), Wilbur admitted to taking the illegal anabolic steroids Trenabol (Cobb County Department of Public Safety Internal Affairs, 2011, page 146) and Deca (Cobb County Department of Public Safety Internal Affairs, 2011, page 147), knowing that each was an illegal anabolic steroid (Cobb County Department of Public Safety Internal Affairs file 11-00010, p. 156) and lying to investigators previously (Cobb County Department of Public Safety Internal Affairs, 2011, pp. 152, 162).

Wilbur resigned from the fire department on May 6, 2011, before the results of his May 4, 2011, drug test results for steroids were available (Cobb County Department of Public Safety Internal Affairs,

2011, p. 005). It was only after the drug test that Wilbur returned to tell the truth. Wilbur's drug test results showed he was positive for illegal anabolic steroids, Boldenone and Nandrolone (Cobb County Internal Affairs, 2011, p. 51). However, his story continues at a new fire department.

Wilbur moved around to other agencies and finally settled with the Smyrna Fire Department in Georgia. Soon, he came to the attention of internal affairs investigators in the city. Wilbur was found in possession of "….a number of syringes, vials and pills as follows: the vials containing a liquid were of different sizes and were marked as either "Stanozolol", "Sustanon", "Ondansetron", or "Drostanolone Propionate", there was a small bottle of "Nitrostatc" (nitroglycerine) tablets," and the pills Wilbur had on October 17, 2012, included, "seven pills marked "Ondansetron" in bubble packs, and an unmarked pill bottle with two separate pills inside,"…the drugs were confiscated (Smyrna Police Department Internal Affairs Report, 2012, p. 3). A second Internal Investigation was conducted by Smyrna Police Department. This second clarified issues surrounding Phillip Wilbur.

"Deputy Chief Acree (Smyrna Fire Department) said he was present when Wilbur removed the two bags from his vehicle and gave them to Lt. Johnson…Deputy Chief Acree said he was also present when Chief Lanyon (Smyrna Fire Department) talked with Wilbur and, when it appeared he was going to return Wilbur to full duty, D.C. Acree spoke to Chief Lanyon in private and pointed out that Wilbur needed to be fired because he was in possession of illegal drugs while on duty. Chief Lanyon agreed and called Wilbur back into the office and gave him the chance to resign in lieu of termination, in which he did resign" (Smyrna Police Department Internal Affairs Report, 2013, p. 2).

The second report indicates Wilbur should have been charged with multiple felony counts of illegal possession of Schedule III anabolic steroids: Stanozolol, Sustanon, and felony possession (e.g., possession with intent to deliver) of other drugs for which he had no prescription: Ondansetron (liquid), Ondansetron (pills), and Nitrostat.

Instead, and to the amazement of the authors, this cache of illegal steroids was returned to Wilbur from the evidence room of the police department after he resigned. On November 12, 2012, Phillip Wilbur was allowed to sign his illegal steroids out of the Smyrna Police

Department Evidence Room and went off to work for another fire department in Georgia. Despite internal affairs investigations that revealed related administrative misconduct, none of those involved have been charged with any crime. In addition, both the Georgia Bureau of Investigation and the FBI have refused to investigate the case because they claim it is not within their current parameters. However, both agencies agree that crimes have been committed.

As of this writing, Phillip Wilbur has been arrested for forgery in relation to falsifying his drug test results in a civil matter. However, he continues to give false testimony regarding his arrest history, his history of steroid abuse, and his history of dealing. And no judge has held him to account for these lies, despite acknowledging them and promising to do so.

To be clear: Each of the individuals named in this scandal identified Wilbur as their drug dealer and as an illegal drug user. Each of these individuals also made it clear that illegal steroid use is rampant in Public Safety throughout Georgia. This was confirmed by Wilbur. None have been charged with any crime. In addition, the intelligence and direct evidence of criminal activity related to these cases were provided to state law enforcement (Georgia Bureau of Investigation) and federal authorities (Atlanta-Carolinas High Intensity Drug Trafficking Area—HIDTA office; and the Atlanta Field office of the Federal Bureau of Investigation). To our knowledge, no investigation has taken place; certainly, no one has been arrested.

If any of these individuals is taken to trial for their crimes, it will draw in and expose corruption throughout public safety in the State of Georgia to the point that it would be decimated and therefore crippled. For this reason, and to maintain the image of local public safety, the authors believe that there is no incentive to bring any of these individuals to justice. This also means that there is no incentive to identify others in public safety as criminal participants. As such, there appears no remedy in the criminal justice system for these crimes, and others are likely to suffer harm because of them.

7.6 CONCLUSION

These cases evidence a pattern of anabolic steroid abuse that spans all manner of public safety agencies. They also evidence a pattern of willful negligence and criminal misconduct by not only public safety employees, but their coworkers, supervisors, and the leadership in general. There are three parts to the problem: those committing the crimes of abuse and distribution; those willfully ignoring the crimes that they see (coworkers and family members); and those failing to hold public safety employees accountable by virtue of arrest, prosecution, and incarceration (investigators, supervisors, and the courts).

Those involved in these cases must be brought to justice in a court of law by the public servants charged with upholding it, and publicly held to account for their criminal misconduct. Unfortunately, this kind of accountability is not always in the best interest of our public safety agencies. Consequently, there are those who commit these crimes, admit to them on the record, and draw maps to the crimes of others but with no real fear of any criminal charges being brought. Instead, they are merely fired, or allowed to resign, and the problem moves on to another agency to perpetuate.

CHAPTER 8

Policies and Reforms

The authors would like to make it clear that no state or federal law can be written to ensure that citizens, or law enforcement, follow the laws that are already on the books. Existing rules and laws tend to serve honest men well. In contrast, they teach the dishonest how to hide what they have done and when to lie about it. Laws are incapable of changing fundamental professional character; they only change the way that liars must lie. The challenge is to rid the criminal justice system of those individuals unworthy of serving in it.

Therefore, any reforms to criminal behavior by criminal justice (CJ) professionals must take place in its leadership and culture. As explained by Crowder and Turvey (2013), this means the hiring and retention of ethical employees, and the sanction or expulsion of anyone contrary. This is a leadership issue from start to finish, and until there are better and more ethical criminal justice leaders in place there will continue to be scandals in every part of the system.

What this means is that there can be no confidence in street-level law enforcement as a solution or as a source of reform. Those on the frontline adapt to the example, and the accountability, afforded by their leaders and supervisors. If they are hired into a culture that is rife with ethical complicity and compromise, then they can hardly be expected to behave otherwise. The authors have found that the opposite is also true. And once they give up their professional and ethical chastity, they cannot be trusted again.

8.1 LIABILITY

Public safety agencies that fail with respect to adopting reforms aimed at identifying, curbing, and penalizing anabolic steroid abuse open themselves up to all manner of liability. This includes negligence lawsuits for the hiring and retention of officers and other employees that are "unfit for duty." This is explained by Humphrey et al. (2008):

> Negligent Retention: Agencies have a duty and a right to maintain fit officers and to protect the public from impaired officers. They must exercise reasonable means at their disposal to ensure that officers are fit. Both national and local standards regarding the use of AASs support the idea that officers abusing such substances could be at risk for impairment and could even be involved in criminal activity related to the use of these substances.

Public safety agencies also have a duty to refrain from other related negligence, such as the failure to train and supervise their personnel. Hiring good people is not enough. They must be taught how to do their jobs; they must be kept up to speed with the latest information and techniques; and they must be held accountable through structured oversight.

However, these authors also warn against taking action against public safety employees without cause (Humphrey et al., 2008): "To act against an officer, an agency must have reasonable suspicion that the officer is abusing substances or must have an agency-wide random drug-testing schedule. Agencies may not single out an officer for 'random' drug testing in the absence of information to suggest use, dealing, and/or impairment." This is an important caveat and one that cannot simply be ignored.

Reasonable suspicion can come in the form of a complaint from a reliable source; from observing the officer's conduct (e.g., drug screening should be automatic when the officer is involved in an accident, a shooting, or suspected criminal activity); or from an officer's appearance and demeanor.

There must also be a clear drug policy in place, that is explained to all employees, so that everyone understands it. This includes the supervisors and leadership responsible for effecting it.

8.2 REFORMS

The authors propose the following basic reforms to the problem of anabolic steroid abuse among public safety personnel. However, in order to be effective, they must be administered with haste, with courage, and without exception[1].

---

[1]If these reforms sound like a lot of work, it is because they are meant to. However, this is nothing compared to the future harm and liability that can be avoided. The hiring and retention of those that violate the laws that they are meant to uphold must be considered an unthinkable proposition by any public safety leader (Daley and Ellis, 1994).

8.2.1 Drug Screens for All Applicants

All applicants should be required to sign a waiver agreeing to participate in drug screening during the application and interview process,
and then again subsequent to hiring.[2] This can be done in conjunction
with their physical examinations. This must include a drug panel that
screens for psychotropic medications and anabolic steroids. Testing
hot for illegal substances during these screens should result in criminal
investigations and arrests when illegal drug abuse is determined.

8.2.2 Drug Screens for All New Hires

All new hires should be required to submit to a secondary round of
drug screening, to include a panel that tests for all illicit substances,
including anabolic steroids. Failure of these drug screens should result
in criminal investigations and arrests when illegal drug abuse is determined. It should go without saying that this involves immediate suspension, and then termination upon conviction.

8.2.3 Basic Instruction on Law Enforcement Ethics and Drug Abuse

All new hires must be required to attend a basic course that lays out
their professional and ethical obligations as a public safety officer.
This should include a section on drug abuse and addiction (e.g., alcohol abuse, prescription drug addiction, and street drug abuse). The
adverse side effects, illegality, and consequences of anabolic steroid
abuse should feature prominently. The agency's drug policies should
also be spelled out in a clear fashion.

8.2.4 Have a Zero Tolerance Drug Use Policy

If any public safety employee is reported to, or reasonably suspected
of, illegal drug use of any kind, they should be tested. Failure of that
test should result in immediate suspension and then termination if illegal drug use is verified. This policy must be made crystal clear and
enforced publicly, with shaming in the press, to have any effect.

---

[2]Unionized agencies may have some problems with this. Additionally, drug tests may not be
administered in some agencies until there is a job offer on the table. However, a waiver could be
drafted in order to satisfy these issues. Refusal to sign the waiver would indicate that there might
be a problem, and suggests the need for further pre-employment screening.

8.2.5 Attach Drug Testing to All Annual Fitness Evaluations

All employees should be required to submit to an annual fitness evaluation. This must include a drug screen to be of any value. Again, this must include anabolic steroids.

8.2.6 Lead by Example

Chiefs and supervisors should submit themselves to annual drug testing, to include an anabolic steroid panel, with public results. In this way, they can set the ethical tone for the entire department by their transparent example. They can also head off any criticisms of departmental drug testing policies.

8.2.7 Investigate Roid Mills

If a roid mill is suspected to be in operation, open up an investigation that is thorough, and rolls up the entire supply and distribution chain. This includes locking up anyone that is illegally procuring or prescribing anabolic steroids. Likely this will require cooperating with federal agencies such as the FBI and the DEA. This is actually a good thing, as local departmental politics will then be removed from the equation to the extent that this is possible.

8.2.8 Send Out a Memo Letting Everyone Know About Departmental Drug Testing Policies

The authors wholly concur with the New Jersey AG's Office suggestion that leadership send out an agency-wide memo that spells out the federal and local laws and statutes governing illegal drug use, listing anabolic steroids among them. This along with written agency policies regarding illegal drug use, spelling out the administrative and criminal penalties for those that do not abide. The AG's recommendation reads as follows (AGSSG, 2011, pp. 29–30):

> ***Distribute law enforcement wide letter/memorandum advising all members of law enforcement of changes to the Drug Testing Policy and penalties for improper acquisition of these prescription drugs.*** *Once changes to the Drug Testing Policy are adopted, we recommend that you issue a law enforcement-wide directive clearly advising all members of the public safety community about the changes to the Policy and more generally, that: (1) anabolic steroids are a Schedule III CDS with limited appropriate medical uses; (2) HGH has limited, FDA-approved uses; and (3) HCG is understood to be a masking agent in men abusing steroids and that improper acquisition of any of these substances is both a federal and a state crime punishable, in some cases, with prison time. Moreover, the letter or memorandum should clearly state that we will aggressively prosecute individuals suspected of attempting to, or acquiring these medications improperly.*

8.2.9 Database Roid Mills, Doctors, and Abusers

As with any other form of illegal drug use, law enforcement agencies should create a database of anabolic steroid prescribers, suspected roid mills, and illegal anabolic steroid users. This information can then be used to guide investigative efforts and even shared with other agencies. It also makes a record of criminal and suspect behavior that can be referenced in future investigations.

8.3 TIERED RESPONSES

The authors recognize that tiered responses are necessary to protect the rights of public safety employees. However, it is also important for public safety agencies to respond as they should with any other criminal behavior. Therefore the response should be tiered as follows:

8.3.1 Tier 1—Drug Testing

A complaint of, or reasonable suspicion of, drug abuse of any kind must result in an employee drug test. This test must include a panel for anabolic steroids. These are not generally included, and a specific request must be made. The testing must be immediate and without warning. A positive test should move the inquiry into Tier 2.

8.3.2 Tier 2—Suspension

Any positive drug test must result in employee suspension while an internal affairs investigation is conducted. At the same time, positive test results must be provided to the appropriate external law enforcement agency (e.g., state police, drug task force, DEA) to initiate a parallel but separate criminal investigation. This is to preserve any *Garrity* issues regarding the rights of the employee.[3]

Often, an internal affairs investigation is conducted into crimes by public safety officers without any mention or consideration of a criminal investigation. There is no better way to ensure corruption within a department than by failing to enforce criminal consequences for criminal activity. And there is no better way to ensure that a criminal employee can move on to another agency where their crimes will continue.

---

[3]This refers to the US Supreme Court's decision in *Garrity v. New Jersey* (1967). It provides that during an administrative investigation, a police officer or other public employee may be compelled to provide statements under threat of discipline or discharge, but those statements may not be used to prosecute him/her criminally. Consequently, administrative investigations and criminal investigations into the activities of law enforcement must be conducted separately, and even by separate agencies.

8.3.3 Tier 3—Arrest and Prosecution

If an employee is directly observed committing crimes, such as being in the possession of illegal anabolic steroids or selling them to others, then an arrest must be made. This would include objective records of using and dealing provided by a third party (e.g., photos, videos, phone chats, etc.). Then a criminal investigation must be opened and conducted, and any substantiated charges referred to the local prosecutor.

The failure of a public safety employee to act on this kind of information is not only negligence with respect to official duties, it may also be considered malfeasance. *Malfeasance* is the commission of an unlawful act during the performance of official duties that has an impact on the performance of those duties.

The consequences should be the same as when law enforcement ignores crimes (e.g., failure to report or to intervene) they have observed being committed by those outside the employment of public safety.

8.3.4 Tier 4—Termination

It is generally not advisable to terminate an employee until it can be shown, unequivocally, they have violated departmental guidelines, or they have been convicted of a crime in a court of law. This must be done publicly and in every case. When this happens, others will get the message and fall in line. However, they must be suspended or on highly modified duty up until that moment, to prevent not only liability, but successful wrongful termination actions.

8.4 CONCLUSION

The illegal use of anabolic steroids by public safety personnel is a nationwide problem that is nurtured by distorted law enforcement culture and values. It is further enabled by the lack of preventative and punitive action taken by law enforcement and the courts. So long as public safety administrators and judges fail to confront the problem, deny the problem, or conceal the problem, illegal usage and dealing will continue among the ranks. This will ensure that all of the crimes and consequences detailed in this manual continue to worsen. It will also ensure that public safety agencies continue to incur financial liability as well as the loss of their professional integrity.

It is the view of the authors that these outcomes are undesirable to the ethical CJ professional. It is to these professionals, present and future, that we commit this work. This in the hope that they find the courage to refuse to allow their criminal colleagues to gather, collaborate, and propagate. This in the hope that they find the courage to gather amongst themselves and become the change that is needed in order to preserve public safety as an honorable career choice for future generations of students.

Case Example
Marriya Wright, Deputy Prosecutor, Spokane County, WA

On April 21, 2014, Deputy Prosecutor Marriya Wright of the Spokane County Prosecutor's Office, in Washington State was placed on paid leave pending the results of an FBI investigation into criminal activity.

Deputy Prosecutor Marriya Wright participated in fitness competitions. She shared at least one related bikini photo of herself with Matt Baumrucker while he was incarcerated. This occurred during one of her numerous nonprofessional visits with him. Her high muscle definition, low body fat, participation in fitness competitions, and intimate relationship with this known drug dealer are all red flags for anabolic steroid abuse. Together, they make a compelling argument for departmental anabolic steroid testing.

Details regarding her case were made public in August by the court: she was having an intimate relationship with a drug dealer; was further alleged to be assisting him while there was a warrant out for his arrest; and visited him in jail on personal business, providing him with a revealing photo of herself during one of the visits. Details were reported by Humphrey and Luck (2014):

> Court documents unsealed last week reveal new details about an alleged relationship between a Spokane County deputy prosecutor and an inmate in the Spokane County Jail. The documents include thousands of text messages between the two and reveal the inmate had a picture in his cell of the prosecutor wearing a bikini.
>
> The investigation involves Marriya Wright and inmate Matthew Baumrucker. Baumrucker has multiple felony convictions and even has the word "criminal" tattooed on his forehead. At the time police began their investigation, he was facing drug and assault charges. Police are investigating Wright's relationship with Baumrucker and the possibility of charging her with rendering criminal assistance.
>
> According to the search warrant, Baumrucker and Wright corresponded via text or phone calls 1,280 times between February 6 and March 5. Police found out about the possible relationship while investigating Baumrucker in an assault. On March 3, police were trying to find Baumrucker in connection with those charges. Police say he was at an apartment with a woman who later told police Baumrucker called a woman and said, "Marriya, the police are chasing me, I am in an apartment."
>
> The warrant says Baumrucker told the woman at the apartment that "Marriya told him she didn't have to let the police in to search if they did not have a search warrant."
>
> When police knocked on the door, no one answered. Another witness told police Baumrucker met Wright in a car at a nearby gas station. According to the witness, "she overheard Marriya telling Baumrucker he needed to get his warrants taken care of." That witness says Wright made no attempt to tell Baumrucker to turn himself in to police. Surveillance video obtained by police confirms Baumrucker got into Wright's vehicle at that gas station.
>
> A Spokane County corrections officer was questioned in the investigation and told police Wright visited Baumrucker in the jail several times. Their visits occurred in the attorney-client booth, though Wright was not assigned to any of Baumrucker's cases.
>
> According to the corrections officer, "Baumrucker does not appear to be posturing himself as he would when discussing legal issues." The booth is set up so that paperwork and other items can be passed between attorney and inmate. The same corrections officer says

Baumrucker had a picture of Wright in his cell and in the picture she's wearing a bikini. According to the warrant, "[The] corrections officer has never seen an inmate in possession of a prosecuting attorney's photograph in a bikini."

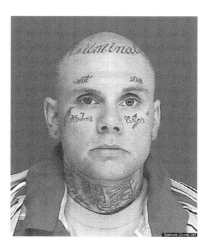

Matthew Baumrucker's mugshot provides unequivocal warnings to anyone considering an intimate relationship with him: the word "criminal" is literally tattooed on his forehead. This criminal background, and his irrational pride in it, makes his intimate relationship with a sitting prosecutor all the more conspicuous and ill-advised for both.

The red flags for anabolic steroid abuse in this case are numerous: high muscle definition, low body fat, participation in fitness competitions, lack of professional boundaries, absence of good judgment, and association with drug dealers in one's personal life. These suggest the strong need for all manner of departmental drug testing, to include an anabolic steroid panel. Failure to conduct such testing would be negligent to the point of reckless on the part of law enforcement.

In September of 2014, Marriya Wright, who is married to a corrections officer, resigned from her post. Her defense attorney explained that "Mrs Wright overlooked Baumrucker's tattoos, was 'trying to save his soul' and bring him into the church" (Boyle, 2014). This defense is problematic at best.

As of this writing, the criminal investigation into Marriya Wright is ongoing, and which includes a public corruption concern by the FBI.

Case Example
Officer Jason Deason and Chief Greg Kroeplin, Canby Police Department and Deputy Jared Gochenour, Washington County Sheriff's Office

In 2008, the FBI initiated a public corruption investigation into Canby Officer Jason Deason. This because of the failure of Canby Police Chief Greg Kroeplin to take action against Officer Deason, who was living with him at the time. Chief Kroeplin was accused of concealing or failing to investigate the illegal procurement and abuse of steroids by Officer Deason. As reported by Bernstein (2009):

Chief Kroeplin was placed on paid leave since Nov. 17, [2008] a day after an Oregonian story detailed FBI allegations that the chief failed to address numerous complaints about former Officer Jason Deason's steroid abuse, enabling Deason to buy steroids on the job and in uniform without any serious investigation...

The FBI investigation launched a public corruption investigation in February, which led to the resignation of former Canby Officer Jason Deason on July 17 [2008].

It also led to Deason's arrest, and the arrest of two of his alleged suppliers, William Jake Traverso,[4] whose family owns Canby Landscape Supply in Canby, and Brian C. Jackson, a former strength and conditioning coach for the Oregon City High School girls basketball team.

Deason, 39, faces a nine-count indictment, including eight counts of official misconduct and unlawful possession of a controlled substance.

John Kelley, City Attorney for Canby, sent Chief Kroeplin the following email, detailing the length and breadth of Kroeplin's misconduct and potentially criminal behavior:

[4]William Traverso reportedly supplied illegal drugs, including anabolic steroids, to police officers, firefighters, and corrections officers.

MEMORANDUM

TO:	**Greg Kroeplin (First Class mail without attachments)**
CC:	**Victor Calzaretta (hand delivered with attachments)**
FROM:	**John Kelley, City Attorney**
DATE:	**March 3, 2009**
RE:	**Due Process Notice**

As you know, the City of Canby has conducted an investigation, through a team of outside investigators, of your conduct in connection with the alleged long-term use of steroids by a subordinate police officer. Based on a review of the investigative findings, the City believes that they support the following preliminary conclusions:

1. You exercised poor judgment 2005 and 2006 by allowing the subordinate officer to live with you at your home for more than a year.

2. You failed to properly respond to allegations in August 2006 that the subordinate officer had purchased steroids while on duty and in uniform, particularly in light of your knowledge of earlier allegations by others against the same officer.

3. You provided false information to your supervisor and in department records regarding the reason that you did not investigate the allegations in August 2006.

4. You showed favoritism to the subordinate officer by not placing him on administrative leave pending an investigation for criminal conduct and public corruption, even though you had placed other officers on administrative leave pending an investigation regarding non-criminal charges.

5. You exposed members of the police department and the public to potential safety risks by allowing the subordinate officer to continue performing his duties without determining whether it was safe for him to do so.

6. You jeopardized the administration of justice by allowing the subordinate officer to perform law enforcement duties and have access to confidential information while he was being investigated for criminal conduct and public corruption.

7. You failed to provide pertinent information to the FBI during the investigation of the subordinate officer, including failure to respond appropriately and with candor to a federal subpoena.

8. Your acts and omissions exposed the Department and the City of Canby to discredit and undermined the public trust by creating the impression of a double standard for police officers who violate the penal laws.

DUE PROCESS NOTICE – PAGE 1

The acts or omissions described above constitute violations of the following standards under the City of Canby's policies and/or General Orders of the Canby Police Department:

City of Canby Policy 11. Code of Ethics

"City employees have a special responsibility to act on behalf of the public good and to ensure that the public's trust in government is respected. Public service requires a continual effort on behalf of employees to guard against conduct that is not only illegal but also conduct that could appear inappropriate to a reasonable observer * * * . Conduct that could appear dishonest to an observer will undermine the public trust even if the conduct is not illegal."

City of Canby Policy 12. Conduct and Appearance of City Employees

Causes for disciplinary action include, but are not limited to, the following:

- Neglect of duty or negligence of duty causing risk of personal injury to the employee or any other employee or a member of the public

- Dishonesty

- Other conduct unbecoming public service or reflecting discredit on the City or any department.

Canby Police Department General Order 1.00: General Rules and Regulations

Policy

6.   Neglect of Duty: Members having knowledge of, and failing to report or take proper action in the case of any crime, disorder, or other act or condition requiring police attention shall be deemed to be in neglect of duty. For disciplinary purposes, neglect of duty shall be defined as failure to give due attention to the performance of duty.

61.   Criminal Conduct: Violations of any law will subject members to prosecution and will be cause for internal disciplinary action up to and including termination of employment. Internal discipline will not be dependent upon the outcome of prosecution.

Canby Police Department General Order 1.01: Professional Ethics and Standards

IV.   Law Enforcement Code of Ethics

"Honest in thought and deed in both my personal and official life, I will be exemplary in obeying the laws of the land and the regulations of my Department. * * * I will never act officiously or permit personal feelings * * * or friendships to influence my decisions. With no compromise for

DUE PROCESS NOTICE – PAGE 2

crime and with relentless prosecution of criminals, I will enforce the law * * * without * * * favor * * *."

VI.   Mission Statement

The mission of the Canby Police Department is to work with all citizens to preserve life, maintain human rights, and protect property; to hold ourselves accountable to our community and to recognize industry standards; to reduce crime, and the fear of crime, by facilitating positive police-citizen contacts.

VII.   Value Statement

We protect the public through aggressive enforcement and intervention activities.

VIII.   Cannons of Ethics

    A.   Canon One

        1.   Peace officers shall recognize that the primary responsibility of their profession and of the individual officer is the protection of the people * * * through upholding of their laws.

        5.   Peace officers shall endeavor to uphold the spirit of the law, as opposed to enforcing merely the letter of the law.

    B.   Cannon Two

        2.   Peace officers shall truthfully, completely and impartially report, testify and present evidence in all matters of an official nature.

        4.   Peace officers shall follow the principles of integrity, fairness and impartiality in connection with their duties.

    C.   Cannon Three

        6.   Peace officers shall not allow their personal convictions, beliefs, prejudices or biases to interfere unreasonably with their official act or decisions.

    F.   Cannon Six

        2.   Peace officers shall perform their duties in such a manner as to discourage double standards.

        4.   Peace officers shall maintain the integrity of their profession through complete disclosure of those who violate any of these rules of conduct,

DUE PROCESS NOTICE – PAGE 3

violate any law or who conduct themselves in a manner which tends to discredit the profession.

7.   Chief Executive peace officers shall accept the responsibility of utilizing all available resources and the authority of their office to maintain the integrity of their agency and the competency of their officers.

G.   Cannon Seven

1.   Peace officers, within legal and agency guidelines, shall share with personnel both within and outside their agency, appropriate information that will facilitate the achievement of criminal justice goals or objectives.

VII.   Professional Conduct

B.   Integrity

The public demands the integrity of its law enforcement officers be above reproach, and the dishonesty of a single officer may impair public confidence and cast suspicion upon the entire Department. * * * An officer must scrupulously avoid any conduct which might compromise the integrity of himself/herself, his/her co-workers or the Department.

D.   Truthfulness

Members shall be truthful when testifying, making reports or conducting any other Department business. * * * Members shall not deliberately make a false or misleading statement to a supervisor or fellow employee.

Canby Police Department General Order 1.02: Department Standards

II.   Policy

In the discharge of duty [an officer] must not allow personal motives to govern his/her decisions and conduct.

III.   Definitions

Affirmative Effort: To self-initiate acceptable ways to comply – to look for ways to comply with the standard rather than looking for the exceptions to the standard.

Controversial Conduct: Conduct which may damage the reputation of the Department or bring it or the member into disrepute.

IV.   Exercise of Police Authority

    A.   Responsibility of On-Duty Officers

On-duty officers * * * are to take all steps reasonably necessary and consistent with their assignment to effect the enforcement of the penal provisions of the City, state and nation and to protect life and property.

VII.   Performance Expectation

Members shall display an affirmative, consistent effort to observe and comply with the Mission, Oath of Office, Code of Ethics, Directives, Rules, Policies, Procedures, Practices and Traditions established for the effective, efficient, and safe operations of the Canby Police Department.

    A.   Work Performance and Practices

        5.   Members will not accept and/or report information related to duties as true or factual without taking reasonable steps to verify the correctness and accuracy of the information.

X.   Official Misconduct

    C.   Conflicts of Interest

Members shall not create conflicts of interest or potential conflicts of interest with the duties and obligations of their positions within the agency.

XI.   Violations of Personal Conduct

A police officer is the most conspicuous representative of government; and to the majority of the people, he is a symbol of stability and authority upon whom they can rely. An officer's conduct is closely scrutinized and when his actions are found to be excessive, unwarranted, or unjustified, they are criticized far more severely than comparable conduct of persons in other walks of life.

    A.   Unbecoming Conduct

        1.   Members, at all times, shall conduct themselves in such a manner as reflects favorably on the Department. Conduct unbecoming includes any act or conduct which brings discredit upon the member, or the Department * * *.

    B.   Controversial Conduct

        1.   Members shall not engage in controversial conduct or behavior, on or off-duty, that brings about public criticism * * *.

DUE PROCESS NOTICE – PAGE 5

Canby Police Department General Order 2.02: Police Administration

V. Command Responsibility

A commanding officer has responsibility and accountability for every aspect of their command.

As Chief of Police, you reviewed and approved these general orders on February 26, 2007.
In addition to the charges stated above, the City also believes that you engaged in insubordination by disobeying the following directives given to you by Mark Adcock on November 17, 2008:

- *Do not talk to any potential witnesses.*

    On November 29, 2008, you attended a football game with several officers in your department, knowing that they were potential witnesses in this investigation.

- *Be available during your regular work hours to cooperate.*

    You left the state without the knowledge or permission of the City Administrator.

This conduct violates:

- General Order 1.00, #54. All personnel are expected to obey lawful orders from ranking personnel as promptly *and as completely as possible.*
- General Order 1.02, V. B. Members shall promptly obey any lawful order of a superior, including orders related from a superior. Failure to obey a lawful order shall be judged to be insubordination.
- City of Canby Policy 12. Causes for disciplinary action include * * * insubordination.

At this time, the City is considering termination of your employment. However, before we reach a final decision regarding whether you should be discharged, we would like to give you an opportunity to appear at a due process meeting to present any evidences and/or arguments on your behalf that have a bearing on this matter.

Please come prepared to provide any information, explanation or other evidence that you believe the City should consider in making its decision regarding disciplinary action, as you deem appropriate. You may be represented by legal counsel in this matter, of your choosing and at your own expense. The City will also, at your request, arrange for the presence of any witnesses who are employees of the City or are otherwise within the City's control to produce.

Although it is the duty of the City Administrator to make disciplinary decisions under the City Charter, we are aware that Mark Adcock was a witness in the investigation and that he may need to participate as a witness at the due process meeting. Therefore, we have determined that it is appropriate for the City Council to preside at the due process meeting and make the decision as to whether termination of your employment is warranted.

DUE PROCESS NOTICE -- PAGE 6

The due process meeting will be held in an Executive Session of the City Council unless you request an open hearing. It will be scheduled at a mutually acceptable date and time that is not less than 14 days, or more than 30 days, from the date of this memorandum. In the unlikely event that we are unable to reach a mutual agreement, the date and time will be scheduled by the City. You will remain on paid administrative leave pending the due process meeting and final determination.

In order to provide you with a meaningful opportunity to respond to the charges, we are providing you with the following materials:

- Summary of the investigation findings and conclusions ("Executive Summary") prepared by Dan Kelly and Alan Corson;
- Exhibits 1-19 to the Executive Summary;
- Audio recording of the investigators' interview with you on December 18, 2008;
- Unofficial transcript of the audio recording;
- Letter dated February 3, 2008 from DA John S. Foote to members of the Canby City Counsel;
- Notes taken by Lt. Tro and Sgt. Green regarding the subordinate officer's behavior in 2008;
- Email communications to and from you in December 2005 regarding the subordinate officer's return to work; and
- Copies of the City of Canby policies and Canby Police Department General Orders referenced above.

Also provided is a copy of an Oregonian article dated November 16, 2008, that resulted in the City's investigation of you. This article is relevant as evidence that your conduct resulted in discredit on the City and undermined the public's trust, and not as evidence regarding the truth of the statements contained in the article.

If you believe that there are additional materials that you require in order to present your case, or if you have any questions regarding this memorandum, please let the City know as soon as possible. If you are represented by legal counsel, your attorney may contact me at 503-266-4021, ext. 254, or the City's outside counsel, Dian Rubanoff, at 503-699-1300. If you are not represented by legal counsel, you may communicate directly with me.

DUE PROCESS NOTICE – PAGE 7

Chief Kroeplin eventually resigned from the department.

Former Officer Jason Deason ultimately pleaded guilty to two counts of first-degree official misconduct and possession of a controlled substance; in 2010, he was sentenced to 120 days in jail and two years probation (Bernstein, 2010).

The FBI's investigation also led them to Deputy Jared Gochenour of the Washington County Sheriff's Office. As reported by Bernstein (2010):

> *Gochenour's steroid use came to light as the FBI investigated the former Canby cop and his steroid suppliers. The FBI found Deason had bought steroids while on duty and in uniform from a Canby businessman, William J. Traverso, and from Brian C. Jackson, a former strength-and-conditioning coach for the Oregon City High School girls basketball team.*
>
> *Once the FBI became aware of Gochenour's connections to Jackson, his own agency investigated him. Washington County Sheriff Rob Gordon found Gochenour had bought steroids while off-duty from Jackson, a "longtime associate" and steroids supplier, violated his oath of office by not taking enforcement action and withheld knowledge of criminal activity from officials once he learned the FBI was investigating Jackson.*
>
> *The sheriff noted Gochenour was assigned to a specialized narcotics enforcement team, and violated the very laws he's supposed to enforce.*

In another textbook example, the 2009 memo from the Washington County Sheriff's Office regarding "Imposition of Discipline; IA 2009-0003" stands out as a document to be read and emulated by departments all over country. It details the nature and extent to which Deputy Gochenour violated his oaths and the law with his illegal anabolic steroid use and related misconduct.

WASHINGTON COUNTY SHERIFF'S OFFICE
"Conservators of the Peace"

Sheriff Rob Gordon **Undersheriff David Hepp**

June 26, 2009

Deputy Jared Gochenour
Washington County Sheriff's Office
215 SW Adams Avenue
Hillsboro, Oregon 97123

RE: Imposition of Discipline; IA 2009-0003

Dear Deputy Gochenour:

Thank you for meeting with Chief Deputy Garrett, Commander Mori and me on June 25, 2009. In that meeting you were joined by WCPOA legal representative Sean Lemoine and the WCPOA President, Murray Rau. The meeting was scheduled to offer you an opportunity to respond to the findings of the above referenced internal affairs investigation. Based on the investigation, and our conversation on the 25th, I have concluded that you violated the following Sheriff's Office policies:

1. 210-R02 § F Neglect of Duty
2. 209-R02 § 2 Drug free workplace (use of controlled substances)
3. 207-R03 § 1 Professional Conduct
4. 207-R03 § 2 Truthfulness (during background investigation)
5. 207-R03 § 7 Knowledge and Enforcement of Laws
6. 207-R03 § 8 Knowledge and Enforcement of Policies and Orders
7. 207-R03 § 12 Withholding Criminal Information
8. 202-R03 § 1 Oath of Office

The facts surrounding these events are detailed in the investigative files. Since the files will be maintained, I will not fully detail the events again in this letter. In summary, however I conclude, in 2007, while employed as a deputy sheriff, you bought controlled substances from another person. The person selling the drugs was committing a felony crime by delivering the controlled substance. You participated in the criminal act, and violated your oath of office by not taking enforcement action. These actions took place while you were off-duty.

I further conclude, that prior to your employment, you were untruthful to background investigators when you told them you had used no controlled substance (other than experimental marijuana). In fact, you illegally purchased and used controlled substances (steroids) prior to your employment with this office. I concluded that you knew your long time associate Jackson, who you also knew to be an illegal steroids supplier, was being investigated by federal law enforcement authorities. Armed with that knowledge, you failed to notify this agency of that on-going investigation, and that you withheld knowledge of criminal activity from appropriate officials.

In deciding the appropriate discipline in these policy violations, I looked at several factors. I note that you have been employed with this agency since August of 2005. Until these events came to light, you were an employee who had consistently met and often exceeded the performance requirements of this Office. You are generally held in high regard by supervisors and command

215 SW Adams Avenue, MS #32 · Hillsboro, OR 97123-3874
phone 503·846·2700 · fax 503·846·2604
www.co.washington.or.us/sheriff

officers in this Office. Your work on the canine team is acknowledged as being first rate. You have no disciplinary actions in your work record and have one citizen compliment recorded.

Seriousness of the offenses. The policy violations you involved yourself in are extremely serious. Law enforcement officers are expected to enforce the very laws that you violated and engaged in while employed as a deputy sheriff. Truthfulness is a cornerstone value for us and other law enforcement agencies. By being untruthful in your background investigation, the veracity of future statements will always be in doubt. It is unlikely that prosecutors would be able to use your testimony in cases you are involved with. Federal officials specifically asked that you be removed from participation in a recent serious narcotics case as they were concerned that your participation would tarnish the investigation and complicate the eventual prosecution of the suspects.

You swore to an oath that you would enforce the laws of Oregon. You did not do so despite knowing that the suspect was a youth athletics coach and could potentially be delivering controlled substances to those youth.

Your core duties as a deputy sheriff include conducting investigations related to criminal activity and appearing in court as a witness. Both of these core functions are compromised by your illegal and deceptive conduct.

I have concluded that the misconduct you were involved in is aggravated due to your current assignment to work with our own narcotics enforcement team. That team is a specialized and elite team that exists to combat any illegal drug activity. I've concluded that your actions were intentional and happened on more than one occasion.

Past practices. Since 2002, nine individuals have been found to have violated their oath of office. Eight of the nine were terminated or resigned in lieu of termination. One received an unpaid suspension of 160 hours. One of the eight terminations was overturned at arbitration resulting in a one week suspension.

Our records show 19 employees who were found in violation of the truthfulness policy. All but one of those was terminated or resigned their employment in lieu of termination. The one exception, was a civilian staff member whose duties do not include conducting criminal investigations, writing police reports, or appearing in court as a witness.

Additional information and conclusions. In our meeting it was suggested that the truthfulness violation occurred primarily due to your inexperience at the time you made statements to background investigators. I understood the suggestion to mean you answered the drug use question based on what citizens commonly think of as illegal drug use. That includes the use of marijuana, cocaine, heroin, methamphetamine or abuse of prescription drugs.

I considered that explanation and once again reviewed your background questionnaire. I noted that the question was very clear – asking if you ever used any illegal drug. You answered that you experimented with marijuana when you were young. Commander Mori listened to the audio tape of your interview during your background investigation and confirms that the investigator asked you very specifically if you had ever used or experimented with any illegal drug. You answered no.

The form instructions clearly state that applicants must answer all questions accurately and truthfully. They tell applicants that negative background information will not automatically result in disqualification. They state that if, after your acceptance for employment, subsequent investigation should disclose misrepresentation, omission of falsification, it may be just cause for immediate dismissal.

I have concluded that your answer was intentionally misleading and in violation of the truthfulness policy. Inexperience or naivety does not excuse it.

In weighing options for final disposition of this internal affairs investigation, I seriously considered your strong work record and your honesty with internal affairs investigators. I also considered that we have invested significant training resources in public tax dollars to your career. Until these violations, you did your job well. However, this decision demands that I assess your ability to continue to effectively perform your duties as a deputy sheriff and make the right decision based on what the citizens and the justice system demand of law enforcement officials. I've concluded that our oath of office and our integrity are not negotiable.

For all of these reasons, I have concluded that any remediation short of discharge would be inappropriate. Termination of your employment is the only option available and is so ordered.

You will be initially placed on an unpaid suspension for a period of 14 days. That suspension will begin on Monday, June 29th. Following that suspension, you will be terminated from this agency. The termination will be effective Sunday, July 12, 2009 at 5:00 p.m.

You may elect to resign from your employment with Washington County if you believe it to be in your best interests to do so. If you choose that option, you must do so in writing prior to 4:30 p.m., Wednesday, July 8, 2009. You are not required to resign and resignation is not suggested. I mention this to you only as an option available if, under the circumstances as you see them, you do not wish to continue your employment with the county.

You are directed to turn over all Washington County Sheriff's Office property to Lt. Cindy Mackley by July 10th at 4:30 p.m. Your final paycheck will be available through Peggy Markos on July 10th at 4:30 p.m.

If you disagree with this action, you have the right to file an appeal in accordance with the personnel rules and regulations or the collective bargaining agreement. You should contact your WCPOA representative if you have any questions.

Sincerely,   Signature Acknowledges Receipt:

Rob Gordon   Jared Gochenour
Sheriff

RG/kmb

cc: WCPOA President, Murray Rau

Approved as to form: Served by:

Paul Hathaway   Name   Date
County Counsel, Washington County

215 SW Adams Avenue, MS #32 · Hillsboro, OR 97123–3874
phone 503·846·2700 · fax 503·846·2604
www.co.washington.or.us/sheriff

3

REFERENCES

ABC, 2007. Wrestler saw his doctor the day he killed his wife. ABCNews.com, June 27. <http://abcnews.go.com/GMA/story?id=3320736>.

Abel, D., 2007. Officer admits steroids charge; Rodriguez also pleads to perjury. Boston Globe, November 20. <http://www.boston.com/news/local/articles/2007/11/20/officer_admits_steroids_charge/>.

ACC, 2014. Use of performance and image enhancing drugs. Australian Crime Commission, Media Centre, January 29. <https://www.crimecommission.gov.au/media-centre/release/australian-crime-commission-media-statement/use-of-performance-and-image-enhancing>.

AGSSG, 2011. The Report of the Attorney General's Steroids Study Group, State of New Jersey, Office of the Attorney General, July 7. <http://www.nj.gov/oag/newsreleases11/Steroid-Report.pdf>.

Augenstein, S., 2014. Passaic Sheriff's officer indicted in alleged stolen-car ring. The New Jersey Star-Ledger, February 26. <http://www.nj.com/passaic-county/index.ssf/2014/02/passaic_sheriffs_officer_indicted_in_alleged_stolen-car_ring.html>.

Benson, R., 2001. Changing police culture: the *Sine Qua Non* of reform. Loy. L.A. L. Rev. 34, 681–690.

Bernstein, M., 2009. Canby police chief resigns. Oregonlive.com, April 14. <http://blog.oregonlive.com/news_impact/print.html?entry=/2009/04/canby_police_chief_resigns.html>.

Bernstein, M., 2010. Federal investigation puts former Canby officer in jail, also snags Washington County sheriff's deputy for steroid abuse. Oregonlive.com, February 25. <http://www.oregonlive.com/clackamascounty/index.ssf/2010/02/former_canby_police_officer_se.html>.

Bopp, W., Schultz, D., 1972. Principles of American Law Enforcement and Criminal Justice. Charles C. Thomas, Springfield, IL.

Boyle, L., 2014. Married prosecutor resigns over "improper relationship with a heavily-tattooed inmate who she sent a picture of herself in a bikini". The Daily Mail, September 11. <http://www.dailymail.co.uk/news/article-2752145/Prosecutor-resigns-improper-relationship-heavily-tattooed-inmate-sent-bikini-picture.html>.

Brittain, A., Mueller, M., 2010. N.J. doctor supplied steroids to hundreds of law enforcement officers, firefighters. The New Jersey Star-Ledger, December 12. <http://www.nj.com/news/index.ssf/2010/12/hundreds_of_nj_police_firefigh.html>.

Brittain, A., Mueller, M., 2011. Booming anti-aging business relies on risky mix of steroids, growth hormone. The New Jersey Star-Ledger, February 14. <http://www.nj.com/news/index.ssf/2010/12/booming_anti-aging_business_re.html>.

Bunch, J., 2010. Denver partygoer's lawsuit says he was "tortured" by cop. The Denver Post, September 22.

Burton, L., 2014. Sheriff fires deputy facing felony charges: Deputy charged with theft from agency, prostituting wife and steroid dealing. Seattle Post-Intelligencer, July 15. <http://www.seattlepi.com/local/article/King-Co-Sheriff-Beleaguered-deputy-fired-5624148.php>.

Buser, L., 2007. Officer charged with drug trafficking: Sergeant lauded for narcotics task force work in '06. Memphis Commercial Appeal, November 10. <http://www.commercialappeal.com/news/local-news/officer-charged-with-drug-trafficking>.

Buttner, A., Thieme, D., 2010. Side effects of anabolic androgenic steroids: pathological findings and structure–activity relationships. Doping in Sports: Biochemical Principles, Effects, and Analysis. Springer, Berlin.

California Crime Laboratory Review Task Force, 2009. An Examination of Forensic Science in California. State of California; 2009, Office of the Attorney General, Sacramento, CA, November. <http://ag.ca.gov/publications/crime_labs_report.pdf>.

Cancino, J., Enriquez, R., 2004. A qualitative analysis of officer peer retaliation. Policing Int. J. Police Strateg. Manage. 27 (3), 320–340.

Cassidy, P., 2014. Barnstable county sheriff's lieutenant suspended after two arrests. Cape Cod Online, May 13. <http://www.capecodonline.com/apps/pbcs.dll/article?AID=/20140513/NEWS/405130329>.

CBS, 2013a. Arlington police officer being investigated by FBI commits suicide. CBS-DFW, June 11. <http://dfw.cbslocal.com/2013/06/11/arlington-police-officer-being-investigated-by-fbi-commits-suicide/>.

CBS, 2013b. Arlington officer admits steroid use. CBS-DFW, July 11. <http://dfw.cbslocal.com/2013/07/11/arlington-officer-admits-steroid-use/>.

CBS, 2014. Former Arlington cop sentenced to a year in prison. CBS-DFW, February 12. <http://dfw.cbslocal.com/2014/02/12/former-arlington-cop-sentenced-to-a-year-in-prison/>.

Cobb County (GA) Department of Public Safety, Internal Affairs, 2011. Investigation Report Number 11-00010.

Cobb County (GA) Department of Public Safety, Internal Affairs, 2013a. Investigation Report Number 13-0017.

Cobb County (GA) Department of Public Safety, Internal Affairs, 2013b. Investigation Report Number 13-0018.

Cobb County (GA) Department of Public Safety, Internal Affairs, 2013c. Investigation Report Number 13-0019.

Cook, R., 2014. 2nd APD officer resigns after allegedly testing positive for drugs. The Atlanta Journal-Constitution, September 15. <http://www.ajc.com/news/news/2nd-apd-officer-resigns-after-allegedly-testing-po/nhNHK/>.

Cowperthwaite, W., 2014. Rodellas busted. Rio Grande Sun, August 21.

Cramer, M., 2009. 11 Boston officers disciplined in steroid scandal. Boston Globe, July 2. <https://web.archive.org/web/20131225033331/>;<http://www.boston.com/news/local/breaking_news/2009/07/11_boston_offic.html>.

Crosby, P., 2009. Doctor sentenced to 10 years in prison for selling illegal prescriptions. Press Release, Department of Justice, Northern District of Georgia, May 12. <www.usdoj.gov/usao/gan>.

Crowder, S., Turvey, B., 2013. Ethical Justice. Elsevier Science, San Diego, CA.

CSAT, 2006. Anabolic steroids. Center for Substance Abuse Treatment, Substance Abuse Treatment Advisory, vol. 5, Issue 3, June, DHHS Publication No. (SMA) 06-4169.

Daley, D., Ellis, C., 1994. Drug screening in the public sector: a focus on law enforcement. Public Pers. Manage. 23 (1), 1–18.

DEA, 2004. Steroid Abuse by Law Enforcement Personnel: A Guide For Understanding the Dangers of Anabolic Steroids. US DOJ, Drug Enforcement Administration, Office of Diversion Control, Springfield, VA, <http://www.deadiversion.usdoj.gov/pubs/brochures/steroids/lawenforcement/lawenforcement.pdf>.

DEA, 2014. Controlled Substance Schedules. US DOJ, Drug Enforcement Administration, Office of Diversion Control, Springfield, VA, <http://www.deadiversion.usdoj.gov/schedules/>.

Federal Register, 2005. Anabolic Steroids Control Act of 2004, FR Doc 05-23907, vol. 70, Number 241, December 16, pp. 74653–74658. <http://www.deadiversion.usdoj.gov/fed_regs/rules/2005/fr1216.htm>.

Fischler, G.L., McElroy, H.K., Miller, L., Saxe-Clifford, S., Stewart, C., Zelig, M., 2011. The role of psychological fitness-for-duty evaluations in law enforcement. Police Chief 78, 72–78.

Fox, 2007. Officials: wrestler strangled wife, suffocated son, hanged self. MyFoxAtlanta.com, June 27. <http://www.foxnews.com/story/2007/06/27/officials-wrestler-strangled-wife-suffocated-son-hanged-self/>.

Garcia, V., 2005. Constructing the "other" within police culture: an analysis of a deviant unit within the police organization. Police Pract. Res. 6 (1), 65–80.

Gardiner, S., 2007. Cops on steroids: baseball has no monopoly on foul balls. The NYPD's own drug scandal keeps simmering. The Village Voice, December 11. <http://www.villagevoice.com/2007-12-11/news/cops-on-steroids/>.

Georgia Peace Officers Standards and Training Council, 2013a. Investigation Report Number 0076831013.

Georgia Peace Officers Standards and Training Council, 2013b. Investigation Report Number 0078741013.

Graham, M.R., Ryan, P., Baker, J.S., Davies, B., Thomas, N.E., Cooper, S.M. et al., 2009. Counterfeiting in performance- and image-enhancing drugs. Drug Test. Anal. 1 (3), 135–142.

Grogan, S., Shepherd, S., Evans, R., Wright, S., Hunter, G., 2006. Experiences of anabolic steroid use in-depth interviews with men and women body builders. J. Health Psychol. 11 (6), 845–856.

Gurman, S., 2013. Denver "gladiator" cop abbegayle dorn resigns amid investigation. The Denver Post, June 11. <http://www.denverpost.com/ci_23438830/denver-gladiator-cop-abbegayle-dorn-resigns-amid-investigation>.

Harris, A., 2000. Gender, violence, race, and criminal justice. Stanford Law Rev. 52 (4), 777–807.

Hartman, P., 2013. Former police detective and his wife sentenced in drug conspiracy. Press Release, United States Attorney's Office, Eastern District of Pennsylvania, January 7. <http://www.justice.gov/usao/pae/News/2013/Jan/gidelson_release.htm>.

Hegel, T., Coughlin, M., 2012. Off-duty NJ cop surrenders after 10-hour Doylestown Twp. standoff. The Intelligencer, June 18. <http://www.phillyburbs.com/phillyburbs.local/tncms/admin/action/%20><http://www.phillyburbs.com/news/local/the_intelligencer_news/off-duty-nj-cop-surrenders-after--hour-doylestown-twp/article_72b6d16a-ed4f-5a79-8427-33983ecdc008.html>.

Hensley, N., 2014. "War Machine" extradited to Nevada for alleged beating of porn star Christy Mack. New York Daily News, August 30. <http://www.nydailynews.com/news/crime/war-machine-extradited-nevada-alleged-beating-porn-star-article-1.1922669>.

Hladky, G., 2012. Steroid abuse has become a major problem among police officers. Baltimore Sun, January 17. <www.baltimoresun.com/topic/nm-ht04ncsteroids-20120117,0,7332982.story>.

Hoey, T., 2013. Phoenix police officer arrested for alleged domestic violence. KTVK, October 14. <http://www.azfamily.com/home/Phoenix-police-officer-arrested-for-alleged-domestic-violence-227755131.html>.

Holland, J. 2012 War Machine heading back to prison for 'some old BS', MMAMania.com, February 3. <http://www.mmamania.com/2012/2/3/2768438/war-machine-jon-koppenhaver-ufc-bellator-mma-prison-jail-porn>.

Humphrey, J., Luck, M., 2014. Court docs: criminal, prosecutor exchanged text messages, bikini photo. KXLY.com, August 25. <http://www.kxly.com/news/spokane-news/court-docs-criminal-prosecutor-exchanged-text-messages-bikini-photo/27718546>.

Humphrey, K., Decker, K., Pope, H., Gutman, J., Green, G., 2008. Anabolic steroid use and abuse by police officers: policy & prevention. Police Chief LXXV (6).

In Re Rodella, 2008. New Mexico Supreme Court, 144 N.M. 617, 190 P.3d 338, Docket No. 31,086, August 19.

James, S., 2007. Police juice up on steroids to get 'edge' on criminals. ABC News, October 18. <http://abcnews.go.com/US/story?id=3745740>.

Johnson, E., 2013. Former deputy faces federal steroid charges. Herald Tribune, October 31. <http://www.heraldtribune.com/article/20131031/ARTICLE/131039904>.

Kappeler, V., 2006. Critical Issues in Police Civil Liability, fourth ed. Waveland Press, Long Grove, IL.

Kleinig, J., 1996. The Ethics of Policing. Cambridge University Press, New York, NY.

KPHO, 2007. Police, firefighters face different steroid standards. KPHO.com, August 15. <http://ktar.com/6/568761/Police-Firefighters-Face-Different-Steroid-Standards>.

Kramer, McGovern, Fay, Bado, Petrillo, Stise, Varga v. City of Jersey City, Jersey City Police Department, et al., 2011. U.S. Court of Appeals, 3rd District, Case No. 10-2963.

Kruse, B., 2014. King County deputy at center of police corruption scandal fired. mynorthwest. com, July 16. <http://mynorthwest.com/11/2566573/King-County-deputy-at-center-of-police-corruption-scandal-fired>.

Lane, M., 2013. Former Jonesborough officer gets 18 months for steroid trafficking. The Times News, August 13. <http://www.timesnews.net/article/9066127/former-jonesborough-officer-gets-18-months-for-steroid-trafficking>.

Lantigua, J., 2014. Former West Palm Beach cop pleads not guilty to selling drugs on duty. The Palm Beach Post, April 17.

Leonard, V., 1969. The Police, the Judiciary, and the Criminal. Charles C. Thomas, Springfield, IL.

Lobosco, K., 2014. FedEx indicted for shipping drugs sold online. CNN Money, July 17. <http://money.cnn.com/2014/07/17/news/companies/fedex-indictment-drugs/>.

Maass, B. 2013. Veteran Jeffco Deputy Busted for steroids. CBS 4 Investigates, September 9. <http://denver.cbslocal.com/2013/09/09/veteran-jeffco-deputy-busted-for-steroids/>.

Maass, B., 2014. Former Jefferson County Deputy gets probation for steroids. CBS 4 Investigates, April 17. <http://denver.cbslocal.com/2014/04/17/jefferson-county-deputy-gets-probation-for-steroids/>.

Marche, G., 2009. Integrity, culture, and scale: an empirical test of the big bad police agency. Crime, Law Soc. Change 51 (5), 463–486.

Martin, J., 2012. Ex-Philadelphia officer admits running steroid ring. Philadelphia Inquirer, October 10. <http://articles.philly.com/2012-10-10/news/34343925_1_keith-gidelson-steroid-sales-christian-kowalko>.

Mayo Clinic, 2014a. Testosterone therapy: key to male vitality? Mayo Clinic website, Sexual Health. <http://www.mayoclinic.org/healthy-living/sexual-health/in-depth/testosterone-therapy/art-20045728?pg=2>.

Mayo Clinic, 2014b. Narcissistic personality disorder. Mayo Clinic website, Diseases and Conditions. <http://www.mayoclinic.org/diseases-conditions/narcissistic-personality-disorder/basics/definition/con-20025568>.

McLamb, S., 2011. Scottsboro mayor confirms illegal steroid abuse among officers. WAFF, November 22. <http://www.waff.com/story/16105675/scottsboro-mayor-confirms-illegal-steroid-abuse>.

McMahon, P., 2014. Former West Palm Beach cop Dewitt McDonald admits selling drugs to other officers. The Sun-Sentinel, June 21.

Mueller, M., 2011. Jersey City police chief wins court battle over steroid testing. New Jersey Star-Ledger, December 23. <http://www.nj.com/news/index.ssf/2011/12/jersey_city_police_chief_wins.html>.

NIDA, 2006. Anabolic Steroid Abuse. United States Department of Health and Social Services, National Institutes of Health, National Institute of Drug Addiction Research Report Series, Washington DC, Publication Number 06-3721.

NYT, 2014. Justice Department Indicts FedEx in a Drug-Shipping Inquiry. New York Times, July 18. <http://www.nytimes.com/2014/07/18/us/politics/charges-expected-for-fedex-in-drug-shipping-inquiry.html>.

Pack, L., 2014. Former Lebanon prison staffer pleads guilty to drug charges. Dayton Daily News, January 28. <http://www.daytondailynews.com/news/news/crime-law/former-lebanon-prison-staffer-pleads-guilty-to-dru/nc48x/?__federated=1>.

Paoline, E., 2004. Shedding light on police culture: an examination of officers' occupational attitudes. Police Q. 7 (2), 205–236.

Perez, A., 2010. Cops' use of illegal steroids a "big problem". AolNews.com, December 26.

Petrick, J., 2013. Clifton police officer sentenced to prison for violent Father's Day standoff. The Record, March 28. <http://www.northjersey.com/news/crime-and-courts/clifton-police-officer-sentenced-to-prison-for-violent-father-s-day-standoff-1.618195#sthash.LS9isaMe.dpuf>.

Phillips, J., 2008. Time for officers to learn martial arts. Houston Police Officers' Union, Badge and Gun, September. <http://www.hpou.org/badgeandgun/index.cfm?fuseaction=view_news&NewsID=423>.

Reed, E., Miller, B., 2014. Motion filed to dismiss charges against Sheriff Rodella's son. KOB Channel 4, August 27. <http://www.kob.com/article/stories/s3544140.shtml>.

SATF, 2009. False reports and case unfounding. Attorney General's Sexual Assault Task Force, State of Oregon, Position Paper, January 22.

Savino, J., Turvey, B., 2011. Rape Investigation Handbook, second ed. Elsevier Science, San Diego, CA.

Schifrel, S., 2010. Staten Island doctor Richard Lucente avoids prison time for peddling steroids. New York Daily News, May 13. <http://www.nydailynews.com/news/crime/staten-island-doctor-richard-lucente-avoids-prison-time-peddling-steroids-article-1.446181>.

Schrock, S., 2013. Arlington police will undergo random drug testing. Star-Telegram, September 15. <http://www.star-telegram.com/2013/09/15/5163379/arlington-police-will-undergo.html>.

Schroeder, L., Coughlin, M., 2013. New Jersey cop gets 8½ to 20 years for Doylestown Township standoff. The Intelligencer, March 28. <http://www.phillyburbs.com/my_town/new-jersey-cop-gets-to-years-for-doylestown-township-standoff/article_14019103-d1e3-5a4d-8872-d6b24d352c0c.html>.

Skolnick, J.H., 2005. Corruption and the blue code of silence. In: Sarre, R., Das, D.K., Albrecht, H.J. (Eds.), Police Corruption: An International Perspective. Lexington Books, Oxford.

Slater, S., 2010. Fort Worth police chief promotes hormone therapy. ABC WFAA Channel 8, May 24. <http://www.wfaa.com/news/health/Fort-Worth-police-chief-promotes-hormone-therapy-94796859.html>.

Smyrna (GA) Police Department, Internal Affairs, 2012. Investigation Report IA 120203.

Smyrna (GA) Police Department, Internal Affairs, 2013. Investigation Report IA 130195.

Staff, 2014. New Mexico sheriff arrested on civil rights, weapons charges. CBS News, August 15. <http://www.cbsnews.com/news/new-mexico-sheriff-arrested-on-civil-rights-weapons-charges/>.

Stephens, N., 2006. Law enforcement ethics do not begin when you pin on the badge. FBI Law Enforc. Bull. 22 (3).

Stiny, A., 2014a. Sheriff Rodella's son disputes details of chase, arrest. Albuquerque Journal, September 25. <http://www.abqjournal.com/468151/abqnewsseeker/sheriff-rodellas-son-disputes-details-of-chase-arrest.html>.

Stiny, A., 2014b. Rio Arriba Sheriff Tommy Rodella found guilty on both counts. Albuquerque Journal, September 26. <http://www.abqjournal.com/469030/uncategorized/rodella-found-guilty-on-both-counts.html>.

Sullivan, J., 1977. Introduction to Police Science, third ed. McGraw-Hill, New York, NY.

Sullivan, J., 2014. Ex-sheriff's deputy pleads guilty to prostitution, theft, drug charges. Seattle Times, August 4.

Swanson, C., Gaines, L., Gore, B., 1991. Abuse of anabolic steroids. FBI Law Enforc. Bull. 60 (8), 19–24.

Sweitzer, P., 2004. Drug law enforcement in crisis: cops on steroids. J. Sports Law Contemp. Probl. 2 (2), 193–229.

Terrill, W., Paoline, A., Manning, P., 2003. Police culture and coercion. Criminology 41 (4), 1003–1034.

Thomas, L. 2012 War Machine reflects on nearly two years of life in jail, returning to MMA, MMAFighting.com, Nov. 7. <http://www.mmafighting.com/2012/11/7/3615712/war-machine-reflects-two-years-jail-returning-bellator-mma-welterweight-vote-fight-news>.

Trenton, J., Currier, G., 2005. Behavioural manifestations of anabolic steroid use. CNS Drugs 19 (7), 571–595.

Turvey, B., 2013. Forensic Fraud: Evaluating Law Enforcement and Forensic Science Cultures in the Context of Examiner Misconduct. Elsevier Science, San Diego, CA.

USA, 2014. West Palm Beach police officer pleads guilty to selling controlled substances while in uniform and on duty. Press Release, U.S. Attorney's Office, Southern District of Florida, April 30.

Vera v. Smith, et al., 2005. Case No. CV 05-1078-PHX-NVW, November 17.

Waddington, P., 1999. Police (canteen) sub-culture: an appreciation. Br. J. Criminol. 39 (2), 287–309.

Washington v. Darrion K. Holiwell, 2014. Superior Court of Washington for King County, No. 14-1-02938-8 SEA, Certification for Determination of Probable Cause, June 19.

Wilairat, A., 2005. Faster, higher, stronger? Federal efforts to criminalize anabolic steroids and steroid precursors. J. Healthcare Law Policy 8 (2), 377–408.

Wiley, N., 2013. Firefighters disciplined in wake of steroid probe. Marietta Dailey Journal, August 14. <http://mdjonline.com/view/full_story/23360253/article-Firefighters-disciplined-in-wake-of-steroid-probe>.

Wolfe, S., Picquero, A., 2011. Organizational justice and police misconduct. Crim. Just. Behav. 38 (4), 332–353.

Printed in the United States
By Bookmasters